Kay Kelly

RIG FOR CHURCH

THE MACMILLAN COMPANY
NEW YORK · BOSTON · CHICAGO · DALLAS
ATLANTA · SAN FRANCISCO

MACMILLAN AND CO., Limited
LONDON · BOMBAY · CALCUTTA · MADRAS
MELBOURNE

**THE MACMILLAN COMPANY
OF CANADA, Limited**
TORONTO

WILLIAM A. MAGUIRE
Captain, (Ch C), U. S. N.

RIG FOR CHURCH

by

William A. Maguire

FLEET CHAPLAIN, PACIFIC FLEET

New York

THE MACMILLAN COMPANY

1942

Set up and printed.

First Printing.
Second Printing.
Third Printing.
Fourth Printing.
Fifth Printing.
Sixth Printing.
Seventh Printing.

PRINTED IN THE UNITED STATES OF AMERICA

To my niece

"BABA" NOLAN

of CASA DE ANITA

FOREWORD

THE manuscript for this book has been submitted to me by the publishers—why, I do not know, unless at the suggestion of my very dear friend Captain William A. Maguire, (ChC), U.S.N., the author. I have no invitation to comment, but in view of my personal acquaintance with the author I think a word or two from an officer of the line of the Navy who has served with Chaplain Maguire will not be out of place.

I note in Chapter 11 that Chaplain Maguire has modestly skimmed over the circumstances incident to his decoration with the Navy Cross. I have unearthed the official report of Lieutenant Commander M. B. McComb, U.S.N., to the Bureau of Navigation on the burning of the *Florence H.* in Quiberon Bay on April 17, 1918, the substance of which is here quoted in part:

I take great pleasure in recommending the following officers and men of the *Christabel* for medals in recognition of their distinguished services on the following occasion:

(A) Burning of *Florence H.* in Quiberon Bay, 17 April 1918.

The *Christabel's* anchorage on the night in question was farther than any ship of the convoy from the *Florence H.* She was riding in 75 fathoms of chain and her engines had been secured for a considerable time when the *Florence H.* burst into flames. The cargo of the *Florence H.* was learned later to be steel billets, powder in bulk and carboys of picric acid. . . . The *Florence H.* burned furiously. As the hatches were blown up in quick succession, great quantities of burning powder boxes were hurled about. These covered a large area of the waters of Quiberon Bay, converting them into a burning lake. Several of the survivors were found afterwards to have been severely scalded about the face and arms by the surface water while swimming . . .

For Distinguished Service Medal

Lieutenant H. E. Snow, U.S.N.R.F.
Assistant Surgeon G. E. Cram, N.N.V.
Chaplain Wm. A. Maguire, U.S.N.
Pharmacist Mate 1/c Louis Zeller, U.S.N.
Electrician (g) 2/c Henry C. Brown, U.S.N.R.F.
Boatswain Mate 2/c Wallace A. King, U.S.N.R.F.
Coxswain Evan C. Van Horn, U.S.N.R.F.

(B) The above named men took the wooden power whale boat of the *Christabel* into the midst of the burning lake which surrounded the *Florence H.* and at great personal risk succeeded in rescuing three survivors. . . . One of these survivors was clinging, unconscious, to a boat of the *Florence H.* which was burning furiously. The crews of pulling boats from other yachts who had attempted to reach this man, the last survivor rescued, were very generous in their praise of the daring manner in which the *Christabel's* whale boat charged the burning mass of powder boxes until a passage was forced. The engine of the *Christabel's* boat was very balky and unreliable; it stalled three times in the midst of the sea of burning powder boxes and could not be reversed. This was the chronic condition of the engine at the time and it was known to the men before they were sent out.

Assistant Surgeon G. E. Cram and Chaplain Wm. A. Maguire attended the injured survivors on all vessels of the patrol and returned with them in the *Stewart* to Brest. A great many of the survivors, in addition to the three rescued by the *Christabel*, owed their recovery to the prompt and skillful attention of Dr. Cram.

Note: If this had been a case of "actual conflict with the enemy" the above named men would all be recommended for the "Congressional Medal of Honor."

After some thirty odd years in the Navy, and having served with Chaplain Maguire directly on the China Station and in the U.S.S. *Mississippi*, and indirectly in Hawaii and on our own West Coast, I can testify to the fact that his service reputation classes him as one of the outstanding service chaplains of his time while he has enjoyed the admiration and respect of all ranks and files.

Padre Mio, as we frequently affectionately referred to him, has given us here a simple narrative of his life and experiences which adds a charming chapter to our naval literature.

To Padre Mio—officer and gentleman, kindly and understanding, efficient and capable, counsellor, friend, shipmate—a snappy navy salute!

BARRY WILSON,
Captain, U.S. Navy.

Washington, D. C.
January 29, 1942.

CONTENTS

INTRODUCTION

Aperitif

In the autumn of 1940 in Pearl Harbor, Hawaii, a few days before I became fleet chaplain of the United States Fleet, Father Walter Mahler, now in the U.S.S. *Astoria*, came in a motor boat to the U.S.S. *Indianapolis*, flagship of the scouting force where he found me in the comforting routine of getting ready to step ashore. He joined me for an afternoon liberty, and we drove over the verdant Pali to the beach at Kailua for a dip in the surf. It was our first time together since the night of the fourth of July when several army and navy chaplains gave me a dinner at the Royal Hawaiian to celebrate the twenty-fifth anniversary of my ordination to the priesthood. Walter remarked that I had spent twenty-three of those years in the Navy. To him, then on his second year in the Fleet, that seemed a long time. As we lay on the sand, gazing out to sea, he suddenly turned and said, "Mac, you ought to write a book."

"A book," I cried, sitting erect and taking off my sunglasses. "About what?"

"You," he replied seriously. "You've been around a lot, and you've got a story to tell."

On board the cruiser that evening, I thought it over. My friends, apparently, had shown patience with my yarns about the places I had visited and the people I had met. Maybe it was worth a try. Having just read Benjamin Franklin's "Autobiography," this sentence appealed to me:

". . . the thing most like living one's life over again seems to be a recollection of that life, and to make that recollection as durable as possible by putting it down in writing."

Although I well knew that I should frequently collide with the unpopular letter "I"—that evening I broke out my typewriter, and began.

RIG FOR CHURCH

CHAPTER 1

Up Anchor

HORNELLVILLE, they called the place where I was born, a town in upper New York. Why they changed the name to Hornell, I have never been told. The town was important as the terminus of a division of the Erie Railroad. My father, John Francis Maguire, was the superintendent of the division, and he was known to a little newsboy at the station as the "man who never smiled." Several years later father and I had a chance to verify this fact when we met the same newsboy on the front porch of his quarters at the Naval Academy. The "boy," in the meanwhile, had become Captain Thurlow W. Reed of the Medical Corps. That afternoon father not only smiled but laughed out loud when he heard about it.

I rather believe he also smiled on the night I was born, for it was just prior to the time the bells rang and the locomotive whistles blew, celebrating New Year's Eve in the year 1890. Dr. Raymond Kelly attended mother, and Bridget O'Connor deftly assisted in the role of practical nurse. Dr. Kelly continued to take a skillful interest in our family crises for many years to come. Bridget often came to our home and made candy for us children.

Father advanced quickly as a railroad executive and as he climbed, he carried his fast-growing family with him.

A year after my arrival, the Erie promoted father to a larger division with headquarters in Elmira. We lived on the corner of College Avenue and Clinton Street; it was a kindly place for children. My childhood, thanks to father's military ways and mother's well-placed sympathy, was a delightful experience. I am sure it was, although my memory, reaching back to when I was four, reveals me in the living room, standing in a starched white Sunday suit, looking sheepishly at father as he glared over his newspaper and warned me, "Keep it clean, young man." It had rained that Sunday afternoon a few hours before I stumbled into a mud puddle. When I hove into sight in the hall, father called me to his easy chair, silently removed a slipper, turned me over his knee and warmly impressed me with the importance of keeping on an even keel.

Father boasted a "gay-nineties" handle-bar moustache which, in later years he trimmed to a neat hedge across his upper lip. He was amusingly vain and punctilious about his shoes and his clothes. He was probably the most carefully self-groomed man I ever knew. In my earliest days I felt he might have gone a long way in the military or naval service. I early realized that father demanded an immaculate house, and mother seldom let him down. He inspected like a battleship skipper; we boys were apprentice seamen. I still find myself picking up papers, even in the wardroom, should I find them in my path. Father always insisted on that. I can hear him yet: "Will, come back, and pick up that paper." Whatever habits I may have today in the matter of picking things up or keeping things in order, which I find increasingly hard to do, were made under his quick eye in Elmira. He had the smart bearing of a marine and he gave orders like a four-star admiral. He made decisions quickly and for the most part, accurately; he had a quick temper and on the surface he was anything but sentimental but he was generous and kind.

Mother was an excellent executive officer; in line with Paulinian tradition, she was second in command and usually proved a successful buffer between the commanding officer and his crew. She had a keen sense of fun; she played well on the piano and sang sweetly. While father, after a hard day in the office or a week of inspection on the railroad, buried himself in Dickens or Scott beside the big lamp in the living room, mother—a bit lonely perhaps —took us noisy youngsters by the hand and led us to the piano where she sang old melodies softly.

When I was six, my athletic parents were bicycle fans. But their enthusiasm for long bike rides over the cinder paths of Chemung County upset Father Bloomer's plans for my early schooling. And mother found a chance to show high moral courage.

One Saturday afternoon father promoted a family bike excursion. He had lately acquired two glistening "Columbia Chainless" machines and chose that day for a shakedown cruise. Of the four boys in the family, Walter and I were the only ones equal to the task of trailing. On our miniature bikes we had all we could do to keep up. We pedaled far from town and got back long after sunset, muscle bound and sore. After we had stowed the bikes in the cellar, father rewarded us for our stamina. "You boys may sleep late tomorrow. Mother and I will take you with us to the ten o'clock Mass." Mother had misgivings; she knew how strict the Sisters were about children missing the

Mass at eight. The next day we felt important indeed, sitting with the grown-ups and hearing the ebullient Father Bloomer sing a Missa Cantata.

On Monday morning, however, in St. Patrick's parochial school, Sister Mary mustered the culprits who had "played hooky" from the children's Mass and stung our hands with a ruler. She was so anxious to expedite the unpleasant job that she failed to give us a chance to explain. From the depths of our souls, Walter and I protested and cried so raucously that mother, passing by on a shopping tour, recognized the familiar sounds and followed the vibrations to the school basement. There she found her children. Instantly she spoke her mind, took her sobbing martyrs by the hand and that same morning enrolled us in Grammar School No. 2. Mother worried for a while for fear Father Bloomer might take it out on dad. The pastor had insisted on the law that all the parish children attend his new school. I have no doubt that Father William Brien is carrying on the good tradition. Father must have made amends in some diplomatic way, for cordial relations were maintained until the day the family moved to Paterson, New Jersey.

When father became superintendent of the New York division of the Erie, he chose Paterson as our home town and commuted daily to his office in Jersey City. On Sundays after Mass, he frequently took Walter and me with him. During the hour father spent over his paper-work, we hopped a ferry for a ride across the Hudson to Twenty-third Street. He always gave us each a nickel for the return trip, knowing of course that we would stay on board the ferry and spend it for candy.

My sister Anita, the only girl of the family was born when we lived on East Broadway across from the Episcopal Church. We moved later to an attractive house on Ellison Street, where at the turn of the century we made use of the vacant lots of the neighborhood, digging caves and building shacks. We played a game called "balsey," a sort of hare and hounds that required us to run our legs off in strange neighborhoods where we were not always welcome. One of the local cops made it uncomfortable for us especially when we raced through back yards and over hedges and flower beds. The chief menace in the plot was a guardian of the law we dubbed "Sneaky" Adams, because we believed he wore rubbers to sneak up on us when we were intent on other things. Little did "Sneaky" know that among those he chased on those Saturday mornings was my especial friend, Jack Grimshaw, a future mayor of the city.

In Paterson, another drastic decision changed the setting of my early education. Father thought the parochial school of St. Joseph's was too crowded. Mother suggested that I be placed in a fashionable Catholic Academy. But after a few weeks there, father, having discovered when he quizzed me that I was the only boy in a class of fourteen, came to my rescue. He rebelled, assumed command of the situation and sent me to be enrolled in Grammar School No. 6. Although father subscribed to the Church's policy of including religious training in the daily routine of school, he was a staunch advocate of boys being among boys and probably welcomed a chance to have me exposed to the masculine point of view. For several years I remained in Grammar School No. 6—a dingy old building

of ugly red brick—but every night I recited the Baltimore
Catechism; and Sunday Mass held its own as the most important event of the week.

I met the Navy when I was a pupil in the seventh grade
of Grammar School No. 6. One day the big school bell
frightened us when it rang in the middle of an afternoon
recitation. The teacher excitedly explained that the whole
nation was honoring Admiral Dewey and his fleet, just
arrived at New York from their glorious victory at the
Battle of Manila Bay. Father, in his quiet way had made
plans, and the next day he put us boys aboard a tugboat
for a cruise up and down the Hudson and a close-up view
of the warships. That night the illuminated vessels in
battleship row became a fairyland. Our tug joined a huge
fleet of magnificent yachts that cruised to and fro, paying
honor to the Navy.

Our host of the tug, Mr. Pilkington of the Standard Oil
Company, asked us boys if we would like to meet Admiral
Dewey. Before waiting for the obvious reply, he exclaimed, "All right, I'll fix it." Walter and I then climbed
to the top of the pilot house where we found a decorative
oil barrel with a golden eagle surmounting it. We hung
on and waited for an introduction to the hero of Manila
Bay. The tub drew alongside the white flagship, *Olympia*,
and our host hailed the officer of the deck. "This is Pilkington of the Standard Oil. I'd like to speak with the
admiral."

The officer of the deck manned a megaphone and
shouted, "Sorry. The admiral's at dinner."

"It's important. I've got to see him."

In a few minutes Admiral Dewey, arrayed in his full-
dress dinner jacket, appeared on the quarterdeck. Our

host, controlling his emotions, congratulated the hero of Manila Bay on his triumph and then reminded him that his flagship was anchored a bit close to a cable. It was evidently a hoax, but the admiral accepted it cheerfully. He addressed his parting words to my brother, who by this time was sitting on top of the golden eagle. "Watch out, son—you'll break your neck." Then he disappeared down the hatch. Thirty years later, I conducted Memorial Day services on board the old *Olympia* in the Philadelphia Navy Yard. The good ship reminded me, in her majestic way, of a pleasant evening.

In the matter of our vocations in life, father said little. He did not encourage us to become railroad men, but let it be understood, when we were still quite young, that we should some day go to college, and he would stress the point whenever our reports cards showed we were slipping. Father had never gone beyond the "little red school house," which probably carried him to the modern equivalent of the higher grades of high school. But he had been a good student all his life, and he mastered railroad management from the bottom to the top.

On several occasions father mentioned Cornell to me and gave me a work-bench to encourage my seeming talent for engineering. My brother, Walter, who later became an engineer, was then attending St. Francis Xavier School in New York. It looked as if he would some day become a lawyer or a physician—or possibly a priest. Father may have been impressed by the interest I took in a manual training course I followed as a freshman in high school. I enjoyed working on the lathes and carving things out of wood. He would ask me to repair unimportant breakages around the house, thinking perhaps I had it in me to become a successful builder.

Mother had other ideas, and she proved in the long run to be right. It may have been her prayers that changed me. She had often mentioned how good it would be were I some day to take Holy Orders. This possibility had never occurred to me. I had met no one who even had a relative in the priesthood. That was perhaps due to my training in the public schools. I saw priests only on Sunday and when occasionally they visited my parents. I found it desirable then to busy myself with home work lest they quiz me on the Catechism. I have always believed that the turning point in my life came at the age of fifteen. It was during the week after Christmas. Mother came down with a severe cold which quickly developed into pneumonia. I was genuinely frightened. Dr. Kelly had been summoned from Hornellsville. That convinced me the situation must be desperate. I felt helpless; there was nothing I could do but stand by to run errands or to take my little sister for a walk lest she disturb mother. I began to pray as I had never prayed before. I went to St. Joseph's Church alone and daily stormed Heaven with my pleadings. During the hours of mother's last night on earth when I lay in my bed in the room above hers, I could hear her heavy breathing. I wept and prayed and wept again. The next morning when we five children were admitted to mother's room for the last farewell, I felt strangely resigned to God's will. She smiled as I embraced her. Perhaps she felt that her wish would some day be fulfilled. It may indeed have been mother's prayers that prevailed and changed me, for shortly after she passed away (a loss that nearly broke my heart), I became an altar boy and served at Holy Mass daily. I missed but few mornings of the year I was a freshman at Paterson High School.

The junior curate of St. Joseph's, Father Paul Guterl, invited me to join the chancel choir—not because I could sing well, but I was just the right height for the spare red cassock some one found in the sacristy locker. One of the younger choir boys was Bert Wheeler, who later became a famous comedian. He was several years younger than myself and his liturgical duties were correspondingly simpler. His task was to hold vertically, while marching and kneeling, a large and heavy candlestick. Even in those days Bert was a true show man. Submerged in the austere tableau, with his back to the congregation, his simplest and most natural gesture made us giggle. It was not easy to explain this to our parents, much less to the celebrant of the Mass, without involving the popular Bert in serious difficulties. Wheeler remained a faithful member of the "Mulligan Guards" for a long run. We talked about those days, years later in New York, in Bert's dressing room of Flo Ziegfeld's new theatre. Bert was one of the stars of "Rio Rita."

In the fall of 1905 I entered Seton Hall Preparatory School in South Orange, New Jersey. It was like living the pages I had read in Father Finn's "Tom Playfair." Seton Hall was in the country; the campus was acres broad with ample room for football, track and baseball which the authorities studiously encouraged. Life there presented so different a picture that I felt I had entered a foreign country. All my youth I had attended matter of fact public schools. This place had the gracious charm of medieval France. The ever-present cassocks of the priests and seminarians fascinated me. It was so unlike Paterson

High School where the women teachers and the pretty girls of our class lent a frivolous note to the stern realities of education. It was fun in Paterson to carry books home for your best girl; and the daily flirtations seemed the most delightful pastime in the world. But Seton Hall was built on different ground. This was a man's world and we felt we were doing exclusively a man's job.

The family moved to Bethlehem, Pennsylvania, when father became general manager of the Lehigh Valley Railroad. It was stimulating to go with him in his private car on inspection trips over the road and to meet his capable associates—all splendid men. One summer I worked on the track as a time-keeper. I lived in a farm house in southern New Jersey when I was not walking the ties checking on the hourly labor of eight hundred sons of Italy. I learned that summer to appreciate how much painstaking labor is required in the interests of a traveller's comfort and safety. Also I met and liked the laborer.

At Seton Hall I acquired a love for study. It was a world of idealism. Except for strict schooling in the liberal arts and philosophy, the courses were not, in a business sense, practical. The students at Lehigh University, which my brother, Walter, attended, called mine a "starvation course . . . there's no future in it." But I liked, when I was not playing on the 'varsity, to busy himself with the classics, ancient and modern languages, history, rhetoric, philosophy and an acquisition of a "gentleman's knowledge" of mathematics. It suited me perfectly.

The day after I graduated from Seton Hall, I told father it was my intention to study for the priesthood. He looked at me as though he had half expected the news and suggested that we take a long walk over the hills beyond

South Bethlehem. With our caps and walking sticks we set
forth to discuss my future. Father, aware of the sacrificial
demands of the Roman Catholic priesthood, doubted I was
mature enough to recognize a vocation. He advised me
to enter Yale or Harvard for postgraduate study and take
a Master's degree. I deplored making such a long detour,
but I agreed. Later that summer my college room-mate,
Walter A. Hennesy, persuaded me to visit Catholic University before deciding where to continue my studies. I
went to Washington and quickly decided that Catholic
University was the right place.

In the fall of 1910 I entered the University and began
studies in psychology under Dr. Edward A. Pace, ethics
under Dr. James J. Fox, and I joined the seminar in
Latin conducted by Dr. John Damen Maguire. I rented
a room in Brookland and enjoyed the fine freedom I rated
as a postgraduate student.

One day Dr. Maguire handed me a periodical and told
me to review an article written by a professor of philology
at the University of North Carolina. It had to do with
the "fata" passages in Virgil's Aeneid. That night I showed
it to my friend, Lucien Coppinger, a law student. "Imagine," I complained, "a fellow telling us exactly what
Virgil meant in these passages. I'm going to see for myself." I angrily studied the professor's article; examined
hundreds of passages; consulted translations in the University library and went to town where I spent hours in
the Library of Congress, and I wrote down my own ideas
on the "fata" of the Aeneid. Pleased over seeing the last
of it, I turned in the paper and climbed into tennis clothes.

A few days later, Dr. Maguire told me my paper had
impressed the faculty so favorably that they approved my

trying for a Master's degree, with the privilege of taking it in one year instead of the usual two, provided I covered enough ground on the "fates" in Virgil's work, and completed two minor courses. The joke was on me. From that day I turned to like a salty man-o-war's man, myself a victim of some strange fate. To make it still more confusing, the students elected me first editor of the monthly magazine, *The Symposium*. Working long into the night, I managed to get out three numbers before June. It was interesting but nerve-straining. As the days wore on, I felt an urge to be on my way to the Seminary. My professors talked me out of going to Rome for theology. They favored the chance Louvain gave for travel and language study. The rector, Monsignor Thomas Shahan, suggested that I do postgraduate work abroad after ordination and return to Catholic University as an instructor.

In June father came to Washington and was the first to congratulate me. With a *Te Deum* in my heart, I called on Bishop O'Connor in South Orange and asked him to adopt me as a candidate for the priesthood in the Newark diocese. So everything was arranged.

During the summer the family travelled de luxe in father's private car across the continent to Seattle and down the coast to Los Angeles and Catalina Island. Father arranged to have the car hooked on the rear of the trains; it was quite the *crème de la crème*; he had planned it all like a War College staff officer. He gave as his motive: "Will should see America first."

A few days after arriving home from California, I boarded the liner, *Minnehaha*, with the course set for London.

CHAPTER 2

Under Way

STANDING at the ship's rail that misty autumn morning I saw with my mind's eye a barrier rising and dividing on one side a period of life peopled by family and friends and, on the other, a four-year exile of grim uncertainty. I was not a tourist; none of the exuberance that grips a carefree traveller lifted my harassed spirits. I lighted my pipe, waved farewell with my handkerchief and lay below to unpack.

Wherever I turned, my eyes fell on the word "Minnehaha," embossed on the drinking glasses, embroidered on the linens, and I grinned at it. Minnehaha, "laughing water"—a fine name to give the sea-monster that was carrying me far from my native land. It made me smile, though, and I soon began to take interest in my surroundings.

At breakfast the next morning, still a bit down in the mouth, I listened to a young mother who sat near me coaching her little daughters on the correct way to begin a day. "But, my darlings, you must keep the corners up." The younger of the two precocious children replied, "Very well, mother, but it's hard to smile when you don't like oat meal." I resolved then to "keep the corners up," come what may.

Among the passengers, most of whom were students, was Harold Bauer, a young pianist. We had many good talks as we paced the deck together. One day I found him feeling sorry for himself; and he confided in me. He felt that he was a victim of a peculiar weakness of the American public which required of an artist that he be able to display clippings from continental newspapers, telling of recitals "triumphantly" given in the capital cities. He considered it a waste of time, but he felt he had to go through with it. His first stop was to be London where he would study for a while under a master, and then set forth on his musical Iliad throughout Europe. He stopped at Louvain on his way to Berlin in the late fall and spent a day with me. I believe he is the same Bauer who has since become America's great pianist.

We disembarked at Tillsbury and boarded a boat train that took us to the heart of London. After a few days of sightseeing, and a dinner with Bauer at Simpson's on the Strand, I boarded at Dover a steamer that took me on a rough passage to Ostend. Had I been any sort of a prophet, that trip would have convinced me that I belonged in the Navy. I was the only passenger on board that was not hopelessly seasick. I even had to slink off to the stern sheets to smoke my pipe. The very sight of it drove my shipmates to nauseous despair. I have always been immune to *mal de mer*, thank heaven. I have been able to enjoy my friendly pipe in destroyers when they took them over green and rolled the life-boats under. This blessed peculiarity did not, however, increase my popularity with my fellow officers for most of them were somewhat allergic to the motions of a bucking warcraft.

In the destroyer *Smith* during the war the ship's medico

told me that he had made extensive studies in sea sickness and concluded that only four percent of mankind are totally immune to this unpleasant reaction to the sea travel.

The train ride across the plains of Flanders held my eyes glued to the passing scenes. The long, straight, tree-lined cobble road and the homes that were all alike— squares of red brick built along the edge of the highway —told me I was in Belgium. It was raining, and the peasants, young and old, wore brown capes with monastic cowls flung over their heads. It was bleak but it was Belgium. I made up my mind to become a sympathetic part of it.

I remained overnight in Brussels and took an early train the next morning for Louvain. Its university has, for four hundred years, made the town's name beloved to scholars.

The American College, on Rue de Namur, an integral part of the university was founded in 1857 by two American Bishops, M. J. Spalding of Louisville, Kentucky and P. P. Lefevre of Detroit, Michigan. The College served a twofold purpose of familiarizing American students with the languages and customs of the Old World and of affording Europeans a means of preparing for the work of the ministry in the United States. There were one hundred and fifty students in the College when I arrived. Along with forty or more Americans there were students from Germany, Ireland, Holland, Belgium and a few from France and Italy. University professors came to the College and lectured to our polyglot group in Latin and French. It was amazing how fluently they spoke Latin. It was hard at first but I soon caught on. In the refectory we spoke English, but we took turns speaking each other's mother tongue during recreation hours in the College garden.

An old student friend from Seton Hall took me to town to be measured for soutanes and the other things I needed. It was to be a strange experience—wearing soutane and chapeau in the streets of Louvain, and being called Monsieur l'Abbé Mageer. That was the custom; and it gave the old university town a decidedly clerical color.

I was struck by the variety of habits which identified the many religious orders and congregations of men and women that one met on the streets of Louvain. After a while I learned to know which men were preparing for the missions in Africa; they could be recognized by the thin, stringy beards they were trying to grow. Others, their costume revealed, were to serve as missionaries in China or the East Indies or the Hawaiian Islands. I was affected by this phase of the Church's catholicity. In each specially designed habit there was an answer to an inspiration derived from the life example of some saint of the distant past. Here were sons of St. Benedict, St. Augustine, St. Francis, St. Dominic, St. Ignatius, and followers of many other men who had lived in more recent times. Each saint had his or her special technique for the winning of souls to Christ; each opened a different avenue of progress.

We American College students wore a simple black cassock and a round plush hat. We were to be secular priests in a more general field of missionary work. We were to be in the world and perhaps a little more of the world than the others.

I felt that I was better qualified for the life of a secular priest. It may have been a talk with father that influenced me to make up my mind. He drew a word picture of his ideal. It was a portrait of an intelligent and tolerant person, worldly wise but spiritual, who shared the joys and woes of the people; who baptized the young, trained and guided them to marriage and beyond, as a fatherly shepherd along the rough trails of life. He visualized a priest growing old and white haired in service of a practical kind, of being "all things to all men" in the community. Father imparted to me his aversion to narrowness in any form. In his mind, a priest should be a broad-gauged person, concerned with civic activities as well as interests purely religious. He held that to attain personal goodness in such circumstances, to edify and sustain others by daily contact in the market place, was certainly a worthy ambition.

The austerity of our life at Louvain gave way on occasion to merry social gatherings. Each national group boasted a glee club. The Irish and the Poles added folk dances to their routine. Always on Thanksgiving Day the Americans staged an old-fashioned minstrel show. We often rode out to the College Villa at Sweetwater, a place owned by our Rector, Monsignor Jules De Becker. We had a picnic lunch under the trees and played baseball and other games until the sun went down.

I was singularly blessed, through father's generosity, in vacation time. Whenever I was free to travel he kindly opened the door to the glories of pre-war Europe and I roamed widely and well through Belgium, France, Italy and especially Germany.

I remember especially one day in Munich when I had grown tired of reading German and stopped at a kiosk to buy an American magazine. My eye rested on a familiar purplish cover with the words *Smart Set* inviting me to buy. I bought it and ran my eyes hungrily over the bill of fare. I stopped in the middle of the list at the word, "Beeriad," and on the other edge of the page I read the name, Henry L. Mencken. I thereupon sat on a park bench and began reading "Beeriad." I discovered it was a burlesque of Homer's Iliad, and it took one on a joyous trip around town, stopping where (the author said) the best beer oases might be found. Having nothing more important to do, I set out to verify his predictions and to test his judgment. I carried *Smart Set* with me and read it en route with keen enjoyment. In the last paragraph of the jolly piece I read, "But the best place of all, where the tables are mahogany and the seidel tops are silver, is the Hof Theatre Café. Go there, my friend, and drink a seidel of *Spaten Brau*. And if you should go there, seek out a table in the far corner to the right. There you will be served by the gorgeous, blonde Fraulein Sophie. And don't forget to give her my best regards."

The buxom Fraulein was pleased to hear from Herr Mencken.

Munich was a joyous place the summer before the outbreak of the World War—that bright era which long antedated ugly Nazidom.

CHAPTER 3

I Knew Europe When—

IN THE spring of 1914 we students of the American College were spending a day at the Villa, near Louvain, when a German classmate who had just read about the assassination in Sarajevo said to me: "Mac, that means war." His words had a portentous ring.

One night about that time, I heard a knocking on my door; my visitor was a Russian, a member of my English class. He had come to say good by, for his government had secretly summoned him to join his old regiment in Moscow.

During lecture hours, the rumblings of the caissons as the horses jerked them furiously through the barracks gates across the street, seemed a prophecy of war.

But our academic routine at Louvain was not changed. Students from all over Europe continued to attend lectures together and to play together on athletic teams. Little did they realize what they would be doing a few months hence.

In early June, I was invited to attend the final examinations for the doctorate which were held in the aula of the old library building. The city declared a holiday. Early in the morning, the university band serenaded at the college where the candidates were staying; then came the long and solemn procession down Rue de Namur—mace bearers and professors in their robes, the candidates and the chancellor, Cardinal Mercier. I was the guest of Peter Guilday, now a professor at the Catholic University. He was then a brilliant student-priest, going up for his doctorate in history. The great Cardinal presided. The faculty had invited professors from abroad; there was at least one from Oxford. During the examination of Father Guilday's thesis, the Oxonian asked the candidate why he had not placed a footnote on a certain page of his thesis to indicate that he had seen the original manuscript. Father Guilday assured him that he was quite familiar with the original, and added that he had spent three months in the British Museum. At this moment Professor Cauchie, the famous teacher of historical method at Louvain, and a friend of the candidate, spoke up: "I fear, Monsieur l'Abbé, you spent most of that time in the buffet." His quip was well timed, and it cheered all hands, for the examination which was given in at least four languages, was a gruelling battle of nerves. My friend, Father Guilday, triumphed *maxima cum laude*.

By way of Berlin, Jena, and Leipzig I went to Heidelberg to spend the summer. I decided again to stay in a rectory. There was plenty of room in the priests' house, for at one time it was a Jesuit college. The pastor was a kindly old gentleman, an ex-officer of the Prussian Army. His hair was snow white, but he still stood erect and retained all the chief traits of a company commander.

One night the pastor took me to a student gathering where they were celebrating the end of a semester. When the party was well under way and the songs of Alt Heidelberg rang gayly through the rafters of the ancient hall, a student rose and read a telegram. "Austria declares war on Servia." Loud cheering. He continued to read a telegram addressed to their Korps brothers in Vienna, wishing them luck and expressing a desire to join them.

A few days later, I discovered large posters on display in all parts of town, announcing the plan of mobilization. One afternoon, I noticed the figure 5 written in chalk on the front of the rectory door. It meant that five soldiers were to be billeted there that night.

In spite of it all, they held the annual festival of illuminating the Heidelberger Schloss and students and sweethearts floated down the river under the old bridge singing the praises of their alma mater. It was a touching sight and I now wonder whether it marked the end of the world for lovers of Old Heidelberg.

The pastor prepared well for the departure of the Heidelberg student regiment. He studied scores of sermons that had been preached to armies of the past. He worked far into the night on the sermon he was to deliver at the farewell Mass for the Catholic students. I was present that morning when they marched into the big church. They were stalwart athletes and looked formidable with their heads close-cropped, and their faces taut with the strain of their thoughts. All seven hundred received Holy Communion. I have never witnessed anything more solemn. They must have known that they would be under fire that very afternoon, but they were prepared. It was tragic seeing them march through the narrow streets of Heidelberg—the loved scene of their gay student days. We learned later, when the government permitted lists to be published, that the Heidelberg regiment had been annihilated at Muelhausen.

In a photographer's window, someone had erected a large board on which were pinned each day small pictures of the students who had patronized the place. When a student's death was published on the casualty list, they pinned his picture on the board. It took but a few days to fill all the space, and then it was mercifully removed. It struck me that the older people took their losses deeply to heart. I once heard a woman shout at Mass, "Where, O God, is my son? Give him back to me." The mayor of the town told the pastor that he thought he had lost faith in God when they told him his two student sons had been killed the first week of the war. I could see the poor pastor age before my eyes. He faithfully shared his people's grief.

Most of the American students of our college, all but two of us, returned home during the first weeks of the war. I decided to wait until I received orders to go; it was so interesting that I hated the thought of leaving.

My friend, the pastor, was kind to the French wounded whom we both visited frequently in the hospitals. We wrote letters for them, and the pastor never failed to write to France after burying the poor lads in the cemetery on the outskirts of town.

In the fall I made up my mind to return to the United States, but I felt I should like to see Louvain before I left, in order to make a report on the personnel of the college and university. I went to Mannheim and arranged through the American consul for permission to travel into Belgium.

He, being a professional American, kindly offered me a piece of apple pie. The house was so filled with refugees that we had to sit in the kitchen.

CHAPTER 4

War Zone

IN THE early fall of 1914, a troop train was the only way
of entering the war zone of Belgium. I climbed aboard a
third-class coach in Cologne, lighted my pipe, examined
my papers to make sure that all was in order and then
casually surveyed the scene. The car was packed with
soldiers. They chatted like excited school girls on a picnic
but when they spied me, an ordinary civilian, seated in
their midst, they became suspicious and shouted, "Eng-
lander!" Quicker than it takes to tell it they literally threw
me off the car and my heavy bag after me. I was not to
be thwarted; I had permission to ride, so I climbed into a
baggage car and found a spot in a far corner, which I
appropriated for the rest of the journey, and sat on my
bag. It was in that car that I first heard, from good authority, that the highly civilized German soldier had done
evil things to the Belgians. But I don't propose to go over
here all the unspeakable things I heard on that trip. I
prefer to forget.

We arrived at the station in Liege after midnight and I
tossed my bag to the ground and quickly followed it. The
sequence was reversed this time. I had no sooner picked
up the bag than a tall lieutenant stopped me and demanded
I show my passport. He seemed surprised that I should be

the only civilian in that mob, and a foreigner at that. But he had his orders; he told me to follow him, and he led me to a near-by hotel, watched me register and then told me to wait until he came for me in the morning.

The next day I called on the American consul. He lived in a small house on a side street; the parlor was the reception room and his office was in the rear. When I announced my name to his daughter, who was temporarily acting as vice consul, I heard a raucous shout, "Bring him in!" I was taken through the crowded reception room to the consul's sanctum where that stout dignitary in his shirt sleeves and red suspenders shuffled a heap of papers at a roller-top desk. "So you're an American, eh? Would you like some American tobacco for your pipe? Come over here and take your pick." Then he opened all the side drawers of the desk. In each drawer, packed to the brim, I found a special kind of pipe tobacco. Said the consul, pointing, "That's Bull Durham in that drawer, and that's Barking Dog in the bottom, and that's Blue Boar over there." It seemed to me like good news from a far country, and it made me feel very much at home. When I told him that I was in a hurry to catch a ride to Louvain, for the train would take me no farther than Liege, he leaned back in his swivel chair and sighed, "Stick around. I don't see an American every day. You'll get to Louvain. What's your hurry?"

Waiting there for ten days, I spent the evenings with the consul. Unfortunately he was very lonesome. Our chief amusement was billiards which I played badly, but one evening at his club, a run of luck gave me a fantastically difficult shot just as an elderly man entered the room. He saw my accidental wizardry and congratulated

me. The consul introduced us. Before the stranger left
he made me promise I would take him on for a game some
day. Then the consul, with a hearty laugh, said that my
lucky shot had won the admiration of the champion
billiard player of Belgium. After that triumph I always
found a good excuse for not giving the consul a return
match on his home grounds.

The bread lines in Liege were blocks long, nor did it
help their morale to see cannon and machine guns at every
street corner and on the roofs of buildings.

Finally when I despaired of ever leaving the place, the
consul told me that an official motor car would leave the
city hall at nine the next evening and that a seat had been
reserved for me. It was a big Minerva that seated seven.
A soldier was at the wheel and beside him sat another
soldier who held a rifle at his knee. Among my fellow-
passengers was a Dominican priest whom I had once met
in Louvain. He was dressed in his habit but instead of the
usual chapeau he wore an astrakhan hat with a red cross
sewed on the front. He had been working in the hospitals.
The other two were an army nurse who carried a little
dog in her arms, and a major of the German medical corps.
The medico's face was duel scarred; I asked him why the
universities tolerated so barbaric a custom for it seemed
idiotic to mutilate the faces of the German youth. He
replied, adjusting his monocle, "It makes Spartans of a
military race."

The army car took us through devastated towns.
Though in places the road was in bad shape, we managed
to reach Louvain without damaging the tires. The best
part of Louvain was in ruins. At the American College, the
rector, who had always worn clerical dress, was wearing

a gray suit and a colored necktie. He quickly explained
that the Belgian clergy were in disguise because the Germans had treated them badly near Brussels; a young Jesuit
was shot and more might have lost their lives had not the
American minister, Brand Whitlock, intervened.

When they reassured me at Louvain that I, with four
others, would be given the lectures by university professors to round out the fourth year of our course, so that
I could be ordained the following summer, I returned to
Heidelberg for my trunk and the clothes I sorely needed.
Traveling was more comfortable this time, for the Germans had succeeded in wedging in a few passenger trains.

On my return to Heidelberg I told the old pastor the
story of my adventure. It pained him to learn the truth
and he made me promise I wouldn't tell the townspeople
of my experiences. They still had illusions about their
impeccable army.

Studies were resumed on my return to Louvain. We
nailed oilcloth on the windows of a room on the top floor
where we studied after curfew. Our Professor of Scrip-
ture came on Mondays and we had him exclusively for
three days. Then we concentrated on Dogma for three
days and thus rotated through the curriculum, making up
for lost time and hoping we might be far enough in case
the Allies pushed the Germans out and us into the trenches
we planned to dig in the garden. There was always a
hope that the Germans might be chased out and this helped
us to endure the hardships of the occupation. The Hoover
Food Commission distributed American canned beans and
soup, but I even grew tired of beans.

Some of our former German students came to the
College now and then; they were serving in hospital units

in various parts of Belgium. From them we learned the fate of many of our friends. Some had been killed in battles on the outskirts of town fighting against their former classmates.

No mail came from home during these trying months, but I was able to get word to father that I was alive and thriving, by registering frequently at the American legation in Brussels. Father received the news when the list was posted in Washington. Now and then, with some misgivings, I paid a few francs to have a letter smuggled out through Holland. It was such a risky job for the brave courier that I quit tempting him.

In the spring vacation, I crossed over to Holland and cabled greetings to father adding that my funds were low. I assured the veteran railroader that I was on the right track and that my ordination would take place in July. While in Holland, to escape from the gloom of the war I went to Volendam on the Zuyder Zee and found there the rest I most needed. There would be no Zeppelins flying overhead at night on their way to bomb London; there would be no drunken soldiers to stop me and to run away with my passport when I handed it to them for inspection; there would be peace, for a healthful change.

I attended Sunday Mass in Volendam; all were in their unique costumes; the women, in voluminous skirts and delicate lace bonnets, sat on one side of the church and the men in their tight jackets and wide trousers on the other. They were different from any people I had ever seen, looking like animated advertisements of foreign travel. They were glad I showed interest in their spotless little town.

After Mass I visited the fishing fleet, guided by a group

of small boys dressed in their Volendam uniform of the day. They were agile, in spite of their wooden sabots, and they led me aboard several of the fishing smacks their fathers owned. I wanted to give them a tip for them to buy candy. I explained in my halting Flemish and gave them a coin. They ran off across the cobbled street, sounding with their wooden shoes like a troop of horses, and disappeared in a small shop. Even the youngest of them soon came out puffing on a long cigar. They offered me one, assuring me it was very mild. I tried one of them, waiting around for a while fearing I might have annoyed their young stomachs, but such was not the case. They were veteran cigar smokers. Candy was only for little girls.

I was ordained deacon on Pentacost Sunday in the Cathedral of Malines. We left Louvain at an early hour and made the trip in a horse-drawn wagon. It was considered bad form to ride the German trains unless it was absolutely necessary. My Belgian friends never admitted that the German occupation was anything but a painful interlude. Walking was the chief way of getting from one place to another, and I made many trips on foot to distant battlefields, in quest of souvenirs. I usually went with Milo Verschroegan, a classmate, and he acted as interpreter when I stopped a man and asked for his story of the battles he had witnessed in the neighborhood. Most of the peasants were impressed chiefly by the loud screams of the men when they fought with bayonets. They all agreed it was horrible.

My passport by this time was completely covered with visas and signatures. At a glance it illustrated my wanderings. It showed in official detail how I had entered Belgium

and returned again to Heidelberg only to leave again for
Louvain, and all this during a busy season of troop movements. It recorded my trip into Holland where I might
have been in touch with British authorities, giving them
the benefit of my observations. I found it difficult to re-
enter Belgium after my Dutch vacation nor did I blame
the detectives for treating me roughly at the frontier. It
felt good to be back on the home stretch.

CHAPTER 5

Fourth of July

LIVING under German rule in Louvain was difficult and annoying. In the tobacco shops and other stores there was bitter feeling. People had suffered during the sacking of the city and they were slow to forget. They gradually developed a spirit of defiance which they openly manifested when Germans appeared. I happened to be in a store one day when the girl behind the counter was heatedly reproving a German soldier. He had asked to see pictures of the ruins of a certain section of town; he was particularly interested in that section, he said, because he had taken part in the burning. The girl fixed her eyes on him and cried, "And I was one of the women you took along that night. Get out of here before I kill you." The soldier, dumbfounded, left in a hurry.

It was amusing to see the little children goose-step in front of the artillery barracks across the street from our college. They sang something to the tune of "Deutchland Ueber Alles," but it was a ribald parody in Flemish.

I met several men when they returned from German concentration camps where they had been forced to work for the enemy. Their coats were marked with large numbers. The stories of their sufferings were sickening.

We often played tennis at Judge De Becker's villa on

the outskirts of Louvain. For some mysterious reason we could hear quite plainly the booming of the guns on the Yser Canal. The fighting was at least sixty miles away, but the sounds could clearly be heard and the ground shook so much that the dogs barked. We often paused during a set and looked to the west in sympathy for the lads who were fighting there in defense of the Channel ports. A university professor went to great pains to explain why we could hear the sounds, whereas the people of Brussels, who were fifteen miles closer to the trenches, could hear nothing. He drew on his expert knowledge of geology and made charts to explain it.

At the close of the first year of the World War and my fourth in Europe, we four students of the American College—the only ones left at the university—were invited by the Benedictine abbot to make our retreat for ordination at the Monastery of Mont Caesar which stood on the hill on the outskirts of Louvain. This was welcome news, for I had often benefited by the serene atmosphere of unworldliness which I always found as a guest of the Monks of the West. The monks took pity on us for they thought we had been more exposed to the horrors of war than they. I shall never forget how kind and helpful they were.

Each was assigned a cell and his name was artistically inscribed on a card that was fastened to the oaken door. I carried mine with the legend, "M. l'Abbé Maguire," for many years as a bookmark in my breviary. My companion during recreation was the learned author and poet, Dom Bruno Destree. Here was luck. I had read his books but I knew little about Dom Bruno. Someone had told me he became a Catholic after several years in London, when he was young.

One night in the garden, I coaxed Dom Bruno to tell about his early life. It was not easy, for he said he had lost interest in the days of his pagan youth, and there were so many more important things to talk about. In answer to my persistent prodding he told of the years spent among the literary men of London, of his friends who wrote for the "Yellow Book" in 1894, and of the long nights of song and laughter with Beardsley, Ernest Dowson and the rest. He told of an invitation he once received from Sir Edward Burne-Jones, the famous painter and designer. Destree was invited to dine. During the course of the dinner, Sir Edward turned to the young poet and said:

"You're a Belgian, Destree. Tell us something about Father Damien, the priest who spent his life with the lepers of Molokai."

Destree was confused. "I never heard of Father Damien."

"What, never heard of him? Haven't you read Stevenson's tract, the 'Open Letter to Dr. Hyde'?"

"I can't say that I have," admitted the young Belgian.

"But, Destree," continued Burne-Jones, "you're a Catholic, are you not? I have always thought that all Belgians were Catholics."

The young Destree informed his host that he was not a Catholic. But he assured him that he would read the tract on Father Damien. He kept his promise.

Father Bruno Destree stopped in the garden path and held my arm. "My friend," he said, "I learned all I could about Father Damien and his life among the lepers. That is why I am now a Catholic and a priest." Father Bruno was one of the happiest men I ever knew. He honored me by suggesting that I make the official English translation of his latest book, which may have been his last. It was, "In the Middle of the Road of Our Life." He inscribed it on the flyleaf. The Germans took it from me on my last crossing of the frontier.

I often think, as the warship in which I now serve passes the island of Molokai, how differently it all might have turned out had Dom Bruno been born at Tremeloo and played as a boy with the young Joseph de Veuster. He, too, might have brought happiness and peace to the exiled lepers of Molokai.

Early on the Fourth of July we set out for Brussels. This time we went by train; it was a concession perhaps to the importance of the occasion. We four survivors of our class were to be ordained in the private chapel of the Papal Nuncio, Archbishop Tacci. He became a cardinal a few years later and came near to being elected pope when the College of Cardinals chose instead Cardinal Ratti. The Nuncio's chapel was a gem of art.

I regretted that father could not be there; it was rather a feeling of disappointment; I had no regrets. I was completely grateful and happy. I chose for a motto the words of St. Paul and vowed that I would strive to be "all things to all men."

The Archbishop invited us to breakfast. We sat at a long refectory table. Our host sat at one end with Monsignor De Becker at his right. The Nuncio thoughtfully congratulated me on being ordained on so important an American holiday. "The Fourth of July is an important day in the United States, Father Maguire." I agreed with the distinguished prelate and added the Fourth of July would always be an important day in my life. He spoke at length of the Church in the United States; he knew much about the country and its people as befitted a member of the Pope's diplomatic corps. He invited us American College priests to dine with him in the late afternoon as our train for Louvain was not to leave until late. We enjoyed the hospitality of this true Prince of the Church.

The following morning as was my custom, I served at Mass for Monsignor Ladeuse, the Rector Magnificus of the University. I thought nothing of it but he felt differently when he discovered that one of the newly ordained priests was his altar boy. He helped me with the vestments and asked for the privilege of serving my first Mass. I found his attentive presence of great help. I admired the Monsignor deeply and I felt honored. Assisting also at my first Mass was Father Paul De Struyker, the Vice Rector of the American College. I was indebted to him more than I can say. He helped me especially during the last days when he gave the final instructions on the rubrics of the Mass and other matters of liturgy.

Dressed again in a black suit and a Roman collar—the first I had worn for over a year—I boarded a train for Antwerp. Father De Struyker accompanied me most of the way. On the train I ran afoul of a German officer who objected to our speaking English. "This is a German train," he insisted. "You must speak German."

Father De Struyker was all for appeasing the Prussian and I did not blame him, for he had suffered during the sack of Louvain. The officer came three times to our compartment and chose me for his broadsides.

"You must speak German. English is an insult."

"I am an American," I replied, still seated. "I have permission to ride on this train, and my mother tongue is English. I will speak English."

It may have been the influence of Cardinal Mercier's attitude or perhaps it was pride of citizenship; I remained steadfast and became just as bellicose as the haughty Prussian. When he again returned, puffing with rage, I stood up quickly and with my nose nearly touching his, I looked the bully in the eye and shouted, "What are you going to make of it?"

The trick worked; it shocked him; no thoughts came. But he got revenge by passing the word to his people on the Holland frontier where later the intelligence officers took charge. They tried to prove I was a British spy. My passport confused them; the photograph on it showed me as I looked in Heidelberg, wearing a moustache and a batwing collar and a gay student tie. They found, in one of my two bags, a snapshot of me dressed in the uniform of a Belgian lieutenant, sword and all. I had found the uniform in the College. A medical student left it there when he hurried to the front. It fitted me like a new glove. But here was I dressed as a priest. It bewildered them and they tried to make it all add up to something. During the investigation, which took hours, a brigadier general and his staff entered the room and checked up on the work of the civilian detectives. One of the officers who knew Latin examined the pages of my breviary. He discovered that pencil marks had been made alongside several texts and concluded it must be a secret code. I sometimes wonder why they didn't "bump me off" and have done with it. They were certainly patient and thorough.

Where I stood in the second floor room of the little

station I could see the Dutch train waiting on the Holland side of the frontier. The tops of the cars were painted with huge white crosses. I felt my luck had given out, that the train might leave without me. Finally one of the detectives spoke up. He made a grand speech giving his many reasons for believing I was not a British officer who had recently escaped from Ghent. He said he knew I was an American, that I had all the earmarks.

They at last gave up and ordered him to help me pack and to see that I got on board the Dutch train. We both made a quick job of it. On the way to the train I thanked him and asked why he had done this for me. He replied that he had once been a waiter in Dresden where American families had stayed for long periods. He said they had been generous and kind to him and that he vowed in those days that he would never fail an American in distress. I cannot recall a thing that happened or a person I saw on that ride to Amsterdam; I must have been dazed all the way.

The S.S. *Volendam* of the Holland-American line took me home to the States. My companion on board was a man of my own age named Pyne. He had graduated from Princeton in 1914 and was now returning from our Berlin embassy where he had served a year as a special secretary to the ambassador.

After dinner in the smoking salon Pyne usually distributed a handful of expensive Corona Corona cigars, but he reserved for himself a brand of cigar that looked strangely familiar. When he offered me one I discovered that he, too, agreed with the boys of Volendam: Dutch cigars may cost only two cents apiece, but they are certainly mild. Pyne said that diplomatic immunity from customs enabled him to take back a trunkful. He could not face his father with all those gift Corona Coronas in his bag, unsmoked.

Father greeted me on the Hoboken pier; others of the immediate family were also there and we drove over the Jersey hills to our home in Bethlehem. Dr. Eugene S. Burke, who later joined the Navy Chaplain Corps, and Father Simon Donovan, my old companion on the pilgrimage to Lourdes, attended my first public Mass in the local church. It was an auspicious occasion. I was home again.

CHAPTER 6

Assistant to the Pastor

Bishop O'Connor of the Newark diocese sent me to St. Mary's in Jersey City as my first assignment. I arrived on a sultry day in August with orders to be third assistant to the pastor, who at that time was Father Ter Wert.

It was especially unbeautiful in the environs of St. Mary's. The big, fire-trap tenement houses were down at the heel. All progress, at some distant date, had come to a stop. Even the project of building a new church had not progressed beyond the basement. Services were held there, and the low ceiling and poor ventilation was anything but inspiring to the faithful who came to worship, nonetheless, in droves. Preaching was a feat in athletics. Why the old people clung to that part of town despite the entreaties of their grown-up children, after the latter had become successful in New York jobs, was a mystery I could not fathom. But some were moving out in trickles, finding better places to live on the Heights. This augured ill for the pastor; it was a sort of cold douche on his ambition to build a new school.

Our rectory, however, would have been an asset to any boulevard. My quarters on the third floor were luxurious. I have never since been able to afford anything approaching it. But the sun never reached it. I shared its princely appointments with a parrot and a canary. The latter sang and the former laughed whenever I put the *Il Pagliacci* record on the phonograph, and this helped to create a sort of synthetic sunshine in the place. I was known to some as the "young German priest"—a proof that environment can play tricks on us.

The people of St. Mary's parish were faithful and good. While taking the census, which required stair climbing, I marveled at the way the mothers looked after their many children. With little capital they gave them plenty to eat and kept their school clothes clean and in repair. The boys of the parish were taught by the Christian Brothers. It wasn't easy, but they managed to gain and hold respect and affection. The boys and girls played their games in the streets, and danced whenever the hurdy-gurdy man came accompanied by his aide—a monkey with a tin cup.

St. Mary's was a good school for my future years in battleships. The discipline in the rectory was inflexible. There was a check-off board in the front hall which somewhat resembled the board we have on board navy ships, only it was far more comprehensive. This one had holes in it for every imaginable sortie one might make from the house. A wooden plug informed the commanding officer —the pastor—that you were visiting the school, the convent, the church, the hospital, or just taking a walk or going out of town on your day off; the last hole on the line was under the caption, "vacation." I never found out whether the plug fitted that one.

Services were held every night. After Father Harry Lynch became mortally ill under the strain of overwork, Father Bob Fitzpatrick and I undertook to accomplish all that was expected of assistants to the pastor. It meant that while Bob had the devotion duty in the church, I ran the sick calls. We alternated week for week. During the winter months, hardly a night came that did not find us attending the seriously ill in the tenements. It was excellent training, and it toughened me. If my health had been better, if the war-time food of Louvain had been more nourishing, I might have been able to remain at St. Mary's longer than nine months. But the Bishop knew which way the wind was blowing and he mercifully transferred me to the Immaculate Conception parish in Montclair in the Spring of 1916.

But the people of St. Mary's still had a strong hold on my heart. I had felt useful there. One day a poor lad came to the rectory door seeking advice. I was on duty. He said he was recently discharged from the state prison and that he had found his mother seriously ill when he returned to the backyard shack which they called home. I went with him and found that he had not exaggerated the facts. The mother lay in a dingy room that was indescribably dirty, and she refused to be taken to the hospital; she was superstitious about it. My pleading was of no avail. The next morning after Mass in the convent I told one of the old Sisters about it. She quietly noted the address. I called on the sick woman a few hours later and discovered that the place had been scrubbed till it looked like new. The old lady told me the Sisters of Charity from St. Mary's had been there. She also said that she was willing to be taken to the hospital. That sort of thing was almost typical of certain sections of the parish. The nuns of St. Mary's were superb and the people loved them.

Montclair was then known as the Pasadena of New Jersey. It had much of the charm of the western city, for there were no slums; the people lived in attractive homes. The Romanesque church with its tall slender bell tower was a thing of beauty and the interior was white and chaste. The altars were of Carrara marble and the stained-glass windows came from Munich. When father suggested that I have a chalice made as a memento of my ordination I chose one of Romanesque design. I had seen an ancient one in the Cathedral of Rheims. The Chicago firm of Daleiden made it for me and they said it was made by a Belgian refugee. That struck father as being appropriate. I had it furbished up a few weeks ago, and it now gives me delight to use it at Holy Mass in the Fleet.

The parish boasted an excellent grammar school, conducted by the Sisters of Charity; our graduates did well at Montclair High School, winning more than their share of scholarships at eastern colleges.

In spite of the newness of my position and the responsibilities which were heavy, I could not keep my mind from the European war. I called on the bishop one day and asked to be permitted to join the Canadian forces. I pointed out that I deemed myself equipped at least linguistically for duty abroad. He listened to me patiently and then told me without waste of words to return to the parish and acquire experience. I again bothered him, this time with a request to join the American Army. I felt certain we would soon join the Allies. I nearly won that time; at least the bishop promised to let me go should the United States enter the war. That appeased me. I returned to my parish job with renewed fervor.

It was customary in the Montclair parish to hold an autumn carnival. The senior curate entered his dramatic club with a well rehearsed play. To me was assigned the task of organizing a group of players among the junior members of the parish. There were several talented young women available who fortunately were willing to lend a hand. They did so well that I persuaded them to carry on as a literary and dramatic circle. Open meetings were held every month, and I invited successful women writers to address them. One evening we had Agnes Burke Hale, the sister of my old school friend, Eugene S. Burke. She at that time was editor of the woman's page of the *New York Evening Sun*, quite a position for a young person in her early twenties.

News about our society reached the ears of Joyce Kilmer. He was scheduled to give a reading of Francis Thompson's "Hound of Heaven" at Glen Ridge one Saturday morning and he invited me to meet him there. I was impressed by his simplicity; he was very unlike a story-book poet; I liked him immediately. Having driven to Glen Ridge in a Ford roadster father had given me, I offered Kilmer a ride to the station. We became so interested in each other that we drove on to Newark. I was proud of my Model T roadster, especially when the top was down, affording a fine, unobstructed view of the countryside. It was a fresh, fragrant spring morning; Joyce Kilmer liked it too. Still with unfinished business when we arrived at the Newark station, Joyce suggested that we go all the way to New York and have lunch at the Columbia Club. That suited me, but I hadn't forgotten I had work to do that afternoon in Montclair. It was like playing hooky.

Our first meeting grew into a friendship which involved weekly luncheons. We alternated the place of meeting. When Joyce was host we met at the Columbia Club, then off Gramercy Park. He usually ordered sherry and bitters as an aperitif; and after lunch he smoked his pipe. He had countless irons in the fire and he talked about them, becoming expansive with infectious enthusiasm. He mentioned the names of friends to whom he was devoted, and he insisted that I meet them some day.

When it was my turn, I usually took Kilmer to the grill in the Hotel Astor. It had some of the masculine air of his favorite club, but Joyce was always at his brilliant best when he presided as host in the club of his alma mater. One day he swung to the subject of free verse. He did not fully subscribe to the "movement" which then boasted many adherents among budding poets. It seems Kilmer was an officer of the Poetry Society of America. On one occasion he read a poem in blank verse and said it was written by an ambitious young fellow who sought a word of advice. Kilmer asked that they express their opinions about it. The members unanimously agreed that the poem was a masterpiece. Kilmer confided in me that it was his poem, that he had written it in the subway and that it had absolutely no merit. But it was in "blank verse" and simply had to be good.

It was stimulating to be with Joyce Kilmer; knowing him made me rich with a treasure that only loss of memory can lessen. I saw in him the ideal Catholic layman whose faith and philosophy made him happy, for his every deed was inspired by it. I often visited him in his office in the Times Building on Forty-second Street; he was then editor of the Sunday Magazine section. One day he gave me the galley proofs of his "Main Street and Other Poems" to read. That morning he put through many phone calls to poets of his acquaintance, requesting that they send in their best poems which he proposed to collect for his "Anthology of Catholic Poetry." He asked me whether I knew any Catholics who had written good poetry. I told him I had read poems by a charming old lady of our parish, a Mrs. O'Reilly, and that I would send him samples. I later found one of her delightful poems in the anthology.

On Good Friday of the year 1917 the *New York Times* announced that we had declared war on Germany. After church services that morning I hopped into my Ford and drove fast to the bishop's house in South Orange. The bishop received me kindly. "Well, William, you're here again. I can guess the reason." He gave me permission to apply for a commission as a chaplain in the Army. I chose the Army as the quickest means of going overseas. I sped to Montclair in a daze, and began getting ten letters of recommendation. Father's help got letters from prominent railroad executives and others. But the one I most treasured was a letter from Joyce Kilmer. A Jersey City friend assured me that I would be attached to a regiment in the First Division, so I might have arrived in France with our first troops had I been a bit older. The age limit in the Navy at that time was thirty. This made it difficult to fill the Catholic quota of navy chaplains. Bishops held on to their inexperienced priests. When I arrived in Washington, Father Louis Ahern, the Paulist who represented the Church in such matters, knowing I was only twenty-six, persuaded me to change my application. I returned the ten letters and asked that they be readdressed to the Secretary of the Navy. I was soon ordered to Washington to be examined by navy doctors. The best thing I recall about that first physical examination was that the medicos said it was not necessary to wear glasses constantly, as I had unhappily been doing for eight years. I passed a 20-20. With a salty brusqueness they asked whether I was wearing my *pince-nez* just to look pretty. Their quips were as water to a duck's back. I passed the tests; I was in the Navy!

"Croppy Boy," my Irish terrier, which Father Bogan of Plainfield had sent to me during a blizzard, wrapped up in cotton and snug in a shoe box, I presented to the Meagher family. My old leather chair, into which I had jumped as a child in Elmira, I sent to my home in Bethlehem. I attended a meeting of the Ancient Order of Hibernians where they gave me a chalice and a set of green vestments. I said farewell to all my good friends of Montclair and reported for duty at the Brooklyn Navy Yard.

At last my path was definitely among the waves.

CHAPTER 7

Boot Chaplain

THE gentle Walter Isaacs, a captain of the chaplain corps, ran a "make ye learn" school in the Navy Yard for "just caught" chaplains. His office was on the second floor of an old building and hardly large enough for all his six disciples at one time. This may account for his having kept half his class running errands to the naval hospital and to offices in the Yard. It may also have been his intention to give us practice returning salutes and generally getting the feel of the place.

The black braid on our sleeves which later, by virtue of a change in uniform regulations, turned to gold, and the silver Latin cross embroidered on our collars, told everyone that we were clergymen.

In the morning hours in the chaplain's office, after we had signed hundreds of enlisted men's pay receipts, we picked up bits of naval lore and practical tips on shipboard life. Some of his yarns were amusing, especially when he told of the cruise to Kiel and the day the Kaiser came aboard. But our thoughts were mainly on going to sea; we were poor listeners.

One yarn Chaplain Isaacs liked to tell went something like this:

Years after he had been retired for age, an admiral returned to his old flagship and found to his dismay that she had been modernized. But there was one thing he liked about the new set up—finding his son, a ship's officer, appointed as his guide for a tour of the ship. The proud ensign took his father where the new "gadgets" had been installed. He first led him to the navigation bridge.

"Father," he said, "what do you think of this—all the latest wrinkles—the best bridge in the Fleet."

The admiral cast a critical eye over the expensive layout and replied, "Son, I admire your esprit de corps."

They entered the print shop where a new linotype machine was turning out the quarterly directive. The guide in high spirits exclaimed, "That's something you didn't have in your day, dad."

Again the admiral tartly replied, "You have esprit de corps."

During the rest of the forenoon, in the conning tower, in the forward turret, in sick bay, in the galley, answering his son's superlative praise of his ship the admiral simply nodded his head and remarked, "Son, I admire your esprit de corps."

Just before lunch in the wardroom the executive officer presented the ship's officers. "Admiral Smithers, I'd like to introduce my messmates. They're the best in the Fleet."

The admiral made a little bow and said softly, "Commander Merrywell, I admire your esprit de corps." From the fourth ward came the voice of the admiral's son. "I say, father, what's esprit de corps? You've been pulling that gag all morning." The old gentleman turned to the ensign and fairly shouted, "Son, esprit de corps means the ability of a navy man to lie like hell for his ship."

One day father came to New York and proposed that
we visit a few of his friends in the Fighting Sixty-ninth
at Camp Mills. He wanted to say good-by to Colonel
Hines, a former railroader, and also give me a chance to
meet Father Francis Duffy. Among those in the headquarters tent was Brigadier General Michael Lenihan who
had once been military instructor at Seton Hall. That was
long before my time, but it helped conversation. We met
again after the war when the general served on the staff
of the Naval War College in Newport, Rhode Island. The
last time I saw the general he humbly served as my altar
boy on board the *Arkansas* at Gonaives, Haiti.

It was inspiring to meet Father Duffy, the scholarly and
jovial chaplain. He looked, that afternoon, the chaplain's
chaplain, a true warrior of the Cross.

We were about to leave the camp when a bugler
sounded a call which started things humming. Theodore
Roosevelt was entering the camp accompanied by Colonel
"Wild Bill" Donovan. Newspaper men were on hand for
a scoop. The great Teddy shook hands vigorously all
around, and when he came to where I was standing he
said, "Father, I congratulate you on being in that uniform.
I used to be in the Navy, myself." Then he gave the re-
porters an interview on national war effort, knowing it
would find a good spot on the front page in the morning.

As a grand finale to the afternoon, the regiment marched
proudly in review; they had their hearts in it.

A few days before the Sixty-ninth sailed for France, the
New York Giants got permission to play Monday's ball
game with the Pittsburgh Pirates on Sunday, as a benefit
show for the families of the regiment. It was a charitable
dispensation. A capacity crowd filled the Polo Grounds

and the management reserved a section of the centerfield bleacher for the soldiers. During outfield practice before the game the batter often succeeded in driving the ball over the fence into the outstretched hands of the dough-boys. A cheer went up, for that ball, we knew, would be used on the fields of France.

One afternoon Father Gerald C. Treacy, S. J. came to the Yard. He was in the Army, a chaplain lieutenant. Prior to his joining up he was a member of the staff of the weekly, *America*. That evening he invited me to the home of his former associates where I found the Jesuit journalists typically hospitable. They insisted on my remaining over-night. I enjoyed talking with them after dinner and hear-ing their witty discussions over the long table in the editorial recreation room. The distinguished editor, Father Tierney, presided, and the famous scholar, Father Husslein, was the life of the party.

That night Father Tierney asked me to try to dissuade Joyce Kilmer from enlisting in the Army as a private. He deplored the fact that Joyce would not, in the interest of a promising career, accept a commission in some less perilous branch of the service. In a few days it was my turn to have the author of "Trees" for luncheon at the Astor. He was in civilian clothes and he saw me for the first time in uniform. I wish I had known then it was to be our last hour together. Quickly coming to the point I pleaded with Joyce to accept a commission in the army intelligence service. "It's too late, Father," he said. "I enlisted yesterday in the Seventh Regiment. You must have dinner with me some night in the armory. The beer is especially good."

When I asked Kilmer why he had done this against the wishes of all his friends he gave his reasons. Although the United States did not need him in the trenches, the Allies, by winning the war would bring freedom to Ireland. He wanted the satisfaction of feeling some day that he fought as a common soldier for that cause so dear to him. He added that he would have fought in Dublin in 1916 with his friends, the Irish poets, had he been given the chance. Joyce Kilmer, as everyone knows, was killed in action near the River Oise. He loved justice and freedom more than life.

One evening father and I stood in the lobby of the Hotel Commodore. I had been complaining that Americans were sadly ignorant or indifferent about the armed forces—the uniforms they wore, the insignia of rank, their duties and responsibilities. In the middle of a sentence that had to do with teaching the school children about the Army and the Navy, a sweet old lady dropped her overnight bag beside me and commanded, "Here, boy. Keep your eyes on that. I'll be right back."

Father pretended it was funny, so I told him about Frank Taylor Evans, the son of Admiral "Fighting Bob" Evans. Young Evans was a midshipman serving in one of the ships that visited Newport, Rhode Island, on a practice cruise. After a gala tea at one of the more pretentious summer "cottages," Evans stood at the front gate hoping to catch a ride to the landing. A pompous dowager arrived in her fancy carriage and Evans gallantly stepped forward to assist her. When she was safe on the ground she offered him a quarter tip. Frank Taylor was indignant. "But, Madam, I'm the son of Admiral Evans." The old lady snapped shut her bejewelled bag and glared at him, "I'm sorry, lad, but that's all the change I have."

The "make ye learn course," under the devout disciple of Wesley, came to a sudden stop when orders arrived directing me "to proceed to such port in which the *Maine* may be and to report to the commanding officer for duty on board that vessel." In war times the Navy does not divulge the whereabouts of the Fleet, even to naval personnel. I inquired around the Yard about the *Maine*, but no one would tell. But I learned that the movie agencies in New York were shipping programs in great bulk to Port Jefferson, Long Island, a war base. It was a safe bet the *Maine* was also there.

"Proceed orders" gave me four days for checking out, a fact that reached the ears of Father Hennesy, my roommate at college. When his pastor, Father "Barney" Bogan of Plainfield, New Jersey, invited me to a dinner in New York, I suspected some original scheme was brewing, remembering the last time I had preached in his church. Father Bogan was quite deaf. From the pulpit I saw him standing at the door of the church wistfully gazing my way. At the end he came to the sacristy and said feelingly, "Congratulations, Father Mac, that was the best sermon I have ever seen."

When Father Bogan heard that I was to be the chaplain of the *Maine*, he recalled that his friend Monsignor Chidwick, then Rector of Dunwoody Seminary, had been chaplain of the "old" *Maine*, the one that blew up in the harbor of Havana. Here was a chance to celebrate in joint honor of the chaplain of the "old" *Maine* and the chaplain of the "new." The dinner was a memorable success. The distinguished Monsignor gave me all the "dope" on war-ship life, and Father Bogan supplied the comedy. I knew that Chaplain Chidwick was at his post when his men were killed. As chaplain of the "new" *Maine*, I could not afford to disappoint him. For me it was again to be the slogan, "Remember the Maine."

CHAPTER 8

The U.S.S. Maine

Although my companion on the train ride to Port Jefferson was the genial Frank Harry Lash, whom I relieved last year as fleet chaplain in the *California*, I thought we were going to the ends of the earth. Being still a "boot" the varied pieces of my luggage exceeded my needs; it proved a major task getting trunk, boxes, Mass kit and mandolin to the pier where, like a confused emigrant, I waited hours for a boat to take me off to the *Maine*. One finally came, a coal-burning picket-boat, with a canvas hood rigged over the stern sheets. As I jumped aboard, the boat's crew welcomed me and they tossed the impedimenta into the cockpit.

While we chugged across the white-capped bay, I leaned over the gunwale to catch a glimpse of the vast array of warships that swung at anchor in the distant waters. Beyond the larger and newer ships lay dozens of smaller craft—the *Ohio, Missouri* and the *Kearsarge*—all of the vintage of '98. The *Maine's* three superlatively tall smoke pipes caught the eye. I did not realize then that they had something to do with her appetite for coal. Coaling ship for the *Maine*, an "all hands evolution," came far more frequently than pay day. But she looked good to me; her two turrets were businesslike and her brightwork glistened in the afternoon sun.

The steam launch made fast to the starboard gangway, and I climbed up the ladder trying to recall what Chaplain Isaacs had said about the correct way to board a man o' war. On the top grating I paused and saluted the colors. There was no crucifix there, as in the days of Columbus, but the custom of saluting is still part of the procedure of boarding a navy ship. The officer of the deck, carrying a spy-glass, returned my salute to him, and welcomed me aboard. Addressing him stiffly I said, "I request permission to come aboard, Sir," and then, "I am reporting for duty, Sir."

He read my orders and directed the quartermaster to record them in the ship's log. He then summoned a seaman messenger and told him to take me to my stateroom. I followed the man down the ladder and through the narrow passageway to the steel locker that was to be my home. It was pitch dark in there until I flicked on the light, for there was no air port. A coal bunker came between the room and daylight. What little ventilation there was entered through the courtesy of the opened door. Against the far bulkhead was a high bunk with several drawers under it. Nearby stood a washstand, a desk and a chair. That scene would have shocked a Trappist monk. Across the passageway was the log-room of the chief engineer, and a few feet forward, the living space of his men, known as the "black gang." The place was never free of voices, annoyed or amused, but always loud. When the word got around that the new chaplain had arrived, I became the object of their interest. Most of them were as untrained in navy ways as myself, and they stared at me while I unpacked, without benefit of a mess attendant; he had not "got the word."

It was a strange world, that "new" *Maine*, but I said to myself, "Keep the corners up, sailor," and "After all, war's no picnic." But I couldn't help wondering whether my friend, Father Barney Bogan, had not pulled my leg.

Anticipating the usual dose of ribbing which all men must face when they join their first ship, I went to the wardroom. My landlubber vocabulary was no asset. Referring to the overhead as the ceiling, the ladder as the stairs, the deck as the floor, brought down upon my head many a fancy quip. My wardroom messmates instituted an immediate search for my sense of humor. Being a Celt, there was some on tap; and I drew upon it in self-defense. In our mess of twenty-five or more officers only two besides myself were members of my Church, but I had to wait until Sunday to find that out.

I realized later that the *Maine's* wardroom was typical. The navigator, Lieutenant Commander Edward Washburn, who kindly offered to "bring me up," told me that two topics were barred in all happy wardrooms—religion and the Civil War. Lieutenant Commander Robert "Jam" Lowe, my friendly enemy, ribbed me unmercifully. Several days passed before I discovered it was all a "gag"; that he had announced before I came that he would "turn on the heat" when the new sky-pilot reported. It startled our messmates when "Jam" and I became inseparable companions and daily paced the quarterdeck.

The wardroom elected me mess caterer and treasurer. I was now in charge of the steward and the mess boys. It was up to me to write out the daily menus and to collect the mess bills. Writing to Fred, the chef on father's private car, I told him my plight. His menus were a bit fancy but they gave me something to work on. Occasionally I went ashore with the steward to shop for the mess. Someone complained that the steward was getting too high a "squeeze" from the merchants. One afternoon, returning from a hike beyond Yorktown, Virginia, with Eddie Washburn, I saw on the dock a gunny sack of Lynhaven oysters. A negro boy stood watch over it and allowed they were for sale. I bought the whole sack and had the "bow-hook" toss the oysters into the cockpit. That evening the mess gave me a vote of confidence.

One evening the captain and the officers' ladies came on board for dinner. The wardroom table was festooned with flowers, and one of the Filipino mess boys, with skillful handling of vari-colored rice, printed the word *"Maine"* along the centerline. Our commanding officer, Captain Joseph M. Reeves, who years later became commander-in-chief of the United States Fleet, noticed, in the middle of the dinner, the unannounced presence of the ship's mascot, a goat.

The captain looked my way and whispered, "We'd better get Bill out of here." But Bill was too quick on his feet. He stepped swiftly to the side of Mrs. Reeves, and when she leaned over to pat him, chewed her corsage to a frazzle. It all ran off so smoothly that one might have thought the act had been rehearsed.

Among the *Maine's* mascots was Pete, the ship's cat. He was nearer to the "lone wolf" type than any cat I have ever been shipmates with. He gloried in his toughness, but especially in his knack of drawing an audience whenever he chose to stalk a bird discovered resting on the quarterdeck. It was a common occurrence, whenever the ship was cruising off the Virginia Capes in fair weather, to find Pete putting on an act for the men. He would hide

behind a barbette whenever a bird lighted and then fur-
tively approach the winged intruder. He seemed to catch
the bird's attention and cast a hypnotic spell upon him.
The tired bird, in obvious terror, stood rigid until Pete
chose to give, with his quick paw, the *coup de grace*. We
seldom allowed him a second tap. Whatever Pete's plan
might have been, the first tap merely spun the bird off
balance. Though Pete was a killer, he seemed satisfied to
prove that he could, if permitted to by his shipmates,
destroy the stranger.

One evening after dinner, while the mess attendants
were clearing the wardroom table, a thought struck me.
What a fine ping-pong table that would make. I consulted
Eddie Washburn, but he vetoed it.

"Ping-pong's dead. Don't spring it on the mess, padré,
they'll razz your ears back."

"But," I pleaded, "ping-pong's a fine game and that
table is just the right size." Being stubborn I secretly
wrote to Spalding's and inquired whether, hidden away
in some remote storeroom, there might be a relic of the
indoor sport. It delighted me one day to get a pleasant
letter from the sporting goods firm stating that a present
of a nickel-plated ping-pong set was in the mail. They also
sent dozens of balls. The *Maine* became ping-pong con-
scious. Officers played the game whenever off duty and
they became expert. Our friends flocked over from other
ships hoping for a chance to play. Who knows, that may
have been the beginning of a survival of that pastime, now
known as table-tennis.

As entertainment officer, it was my "pidjin" to organize
and stage the "Happy Hours." The term "Happy Hour"
is no doubt of ancient lineage. It was a composite of box-

ing, wrestling and vaudeville acts. The ship's carpenters built a boxing ring on top side. The audience sat on mess chairs and benches carried up from below.

I usually doubled as master of ceremonies and referee. My chief adviser in this show business was the chief master at arms, a weather-bitten scion of the old Navy. He was of Scandinavian origin and his ways and manner of speech were as rugged as his looks.

While getting things ready for my first production I had him come to my room for a conference. He assured me that the boxers had been weighed in, that all the props were in order; buckets, towels, smelling salts, resin and a gong. He said, "Mebbe you otta have a pie-eatin' contest for a main event. It's a old navy custom." Gladly agreeing, I arranged with the commissary steward for ten pumpkin pies which would be fairly easy to consume in haste. But the sly old salt told one of the bakers to put oakum in some of the pies. It later was obvious that skulduggery was afoot when the sailors strove to "blitz" that toughened pastry. The master at arms had put one over on me.

My debut as a witness of battleship gunnery took place one day in the autumn of 1917 when the *Maine* steamed off the Virginia coast for target practice. We stood on the boat deck when they fired the after turret. The others in the party were as green as myself. The thrill of suspense was like waiting for a football kick-off, and when the guns roared, enveloping us in a cloud of soot from the smoke pipes, we could dimly see dozens of white sailor hats (including my own) flying over the waters like a flock of scared seagulls. The universal shaking-up was so amazing that I marvelled that the old battle wagon was still in one piece.

In the *Maine* I edited her first weekly paper and called it, *The Foretop*. It carried local news, accounts of Happy Hours, poems, jokes, and an editorial. We printed it on board and distributed it after Saturday inspection. This was the first of ten ship and station papers I edited in the Navy. It was fun to practice various types of writing. Being for all practical purposes the whole staff, I practiced front-page journalese, editorial writing, nonsense and serious verses on page two, and sports reporting on the third and fourth pages. I hoped it might lend versatility to my pen. One column I enjoyed doing was "Dere Sheba"—a series of letters written supposedly by a boastful, bad-spelling sailor who recounted his triumphs ashore and afloat to his doting sweetheart. Each letter strove to win one laugh and sometimes succeeded. The letters always ended with a set formula of farewell: "Hopin' your the same. X X smack smack, Your lovin' Hank," or "Al," or "C. M. Strut." The last name appeared in 1924–26 in the Aircraft Squadrons' *Zoom*.

On Sundays we "rigged for church" with an altar which the carpenters built for me, and with several signal flags to cover the ugly corners of the casemate. The first two or three Sundays, through force of old custom when the *Maine* had no chaplain, right in the middle of my sermon they hoisted ashes and raised a deafening uproar but this soon ceased. The ship's band was not the best in the Fleet but they did fairly well for congregational singing of hymns for the "All Hands" service of twenty minutes which preceded the Mass. The men sat on the narrow mess benches and they knelt on the hard deck. It was painfully uncomfortable but I felt that such worship must be sincere and praiseworthy. Men came to make this public expression of faith with only the highest motives; they lacked the incentive of the civilian whose prompting mother or sweetheart might urge him to attend. In spite of the lack of aesthetic appeal, which is so important ashore, the men attended faithfully. Nor did they permit the long fast until noon to keep them from receiving Holy Communion.

I recall our first Christmas in the *Maine*. The crew decorated the old fighter from truck to keel, and the casemates were redolent with fir trees and holly. The ship gave prizes to the divisions that decorated best. At nine o'clock, Christmas morning, we gave out presents from the American Red Cross. Each sailor received a sweater, toilet articles and candy. And in each package was a letter of greeting from a fairy "godmother." Being one of the mail censors, I learned how much the men appreciated those gifts.

The athletes of the ship's company discovered that several of the Fleet boxing champions had come to the *Maine* Christmas morning to assist at Mass and receive the Sacrament. At Communion time I noticed an unusual delay. The men nearest the altar stayed in their places. Then a huge fellow came forward, followed by men of lesser height and weight. They were the Fleet's best boxers. "Gangway, for the champs." There were five of them, ranging from the heavyweight to the little fellow who tipped the beam at one hundred and eighteen pounds. This manifestation of the "Faith of our Fathers" edified the crew. It was an effective type of lay apostolate, and the best Christmas present I have ever received.

In early January of 1918 orders came to "report immediately on board the U.S.S. *Texas*." She had sailing orders to join the British Grand Fleet at Scapa Flow in the Orkneys. And so after some days I found myself on board the *Texas*.

CHAPTER 9

We Join the Grand Fleet

A few days later as the *Texas* was standing out to sea one painfully cold morning in January, Captain Victor Blue ordered all hands assembled on the quarterdeck. He delivered a spirited harangue stressing the importance of our mission and reminding us that we were to enter the submarine zone without escort, that all hands must be on the *qui vive* for signs of submarine attack.

But it was more the weather and the monstrous seas on that passage of the North Atlantic which made us uncomfortable. I have never seen waves so huge and powerful; they tossed the big battleship with crazy irregularity and washed overboard many of our boats and all the drums of gasoline which we knew the Fleet needed at Scapa. Several men were hurt trying to secure topside gear and the executive officer, Commander Timmons, came out of it with a broken arm.

We arrived at Scapa Flow in the late afternoon and immediately rigged for coaling ship. Though it was hard on officers and men we knew the Grand Fleet had to be ready for sea on short notice.

Chaplain Robert D. Workman, now chief of the chaplains' division in the Bureau, came over from the *Florida* to welcome me to the Sixth Battle Squadron, the American unit. My friend "Bob," a Presbyterian, said that our

Catholic church parties had been attending Mass in the British ships and that the squadron personnel would find it more convenient now to come to the *Texas*. He said he would send over a big church party from the *Florida*. The prospect of a busy time in the five ships of the 6th B.S. lifted my morale.

Scapa Flow is a cluster of bays surmounted by bleak, treeless hills. The place then was filled with warships of all types, under the command of Admiral Beatty.

I went ashore in Scapa sooner than I expected. The day after we joined the Fleet a signal summoned me to the flagship *New York* to arrange for the funeral of a Catholic sailor. That afternoon we trudged through the rain and mud to the cemetery. On the way we saw British destroyer men playing soccer in spite of the rain. When they saw us coming they stopped the game, took off their caps and bowed their heads as we passed. The Catholic chaplain of Scapa, an Irish priest, joined the cortège. On our return to the landing he tried to cheer Captain Hughes and myself with amusing repartee. He was an expert "wise-cracker." We gave him a 4.0, which is "tops" in the Navy.

My stay in the *Texas* was not long but I was in the ship when the Grand Fleet got under way, one foggy night, on a sweep of the North Sea. The German High Seas Fleet was reported off the coast of Norway. We set out to intercept them. Over seventy-five ships weighed anchor at midnight and, with lights extinguished, slipped out through the submarine nets. We remained at our battle stations until noon that day. My station was a casemate where I stood watch with the junior medico and stretcher bearers.

The thought of impending action kept us awake, but we got hungry, and they brought food to us from the galley. A few minutes after noon I heard salvos from our secondary battery of five-inch guns. Hurrying topside, I learned that a sub had been sighted off our starboard beam. Whether or not we hit him I cannot say but I liked the cool way our lads manned the guns. In any case, the *Texas* was not hit by anything more lethal than heavy seas which, none the less, are worth a mention.

The *Texas* wardroom boasted an orchestra. Music of sorts came from a collection of stringed instruments. Lieutenant Harry Hill played the ukulele, Major Pedro del Valle, the master mind of the troupe, and I, played the mandolin. There were also fiddles and a few guitars. We practised in the major's room and gave a concert occasionally in the wardroom, stopping only when the executive officer ordered us to knock off and turn in.

A large group of Royal Navy men joined our ship's company during the early weeks of our service in the Grand Fleet. They were experts in communications, sent to us to train our men in the ways of the British. Lieutenant Commander Aylmer, R.N., spent weeks in the *Texas* as a liaison officer between the British high command and our skipper. He "dressed for dinner" by wearing dancing pumps as a mild compromise with peacetime custom. He had been a navigator for over fifteen years, a thing unheard of in the American Navy, where a line officer serves in every capacity, including engineering, to fit him for battleship command.

The Breton patrol needed a chaplain at Brest, preferably one who spoke French. In March Admiral Sims ordered

me "to proceed to Brest, France, via London, England.
. . . On arrival to report to the Commander U. S. Naval
Forces in France for such duty as may be assigned you."

One night at eleven, a small craft known as a "drifter"
came alongside the *Texas* and took me to the British station ship where I was given a room for the night. From
Thurso, Scotland, a train, carrying only navy personnel,
made a quick run to London.

My fellow-passengers in the Channel steamer from
Folkstone to Boulogne were Australian army officers.
They were big, rugged fellows who, I thought, were a
bit quiet and thoughtful. They had already fought in
France and they knew what to expect after reading the
London *Times* about the impending German drive. They
were in for a "show."

On topside I noticed a great pile of seabags, the same
shape as my smaller one. Carefully examining my collection of luggage I decided to keep an eye especially on the
little seabag. It was the last I had packed. In it were
souvenirs acquired in Belgium, my war passport and other
odds and ends I treasured. But the bag was missing when
I rounded up the other things at Boulogne.

Never expecting to see it again, I reported my loss to
the authorities and boarded the train for Paris. Three years
later, on board the *Idaho* in the Pacific Fleet, a letter
reached me from Governor's Island, New York, stating
that seabag No. 17830 had been turned over to the "Lost
and Found Department" of the Army. I wired instructions and the little bag came back to me. It was black as
ink from the booting it got behind the front lines of
France. It bore dozens of leaden seals, and the address
faintly stenciled in the middle, "American Forces, Brest,

France." It took time, but the prodigal bag finally returned to its grateful owner.

The Australians left the train at Amiens in time to meet the Germans as they crashed through that sector of the bloody front.

CHAPTER 10

Base Chaplain, Brest

BRITTANY

Mist is on the bay
And the sun is never glad
To stay.

Rain is on the winds
Sweeping sullied streets
And window blinds.

Men are on the sea
Sailing with the rain
Eagerly.

Women keep the fires
And yearn the coming home
Of sons and sires.

MARCH 9, 1918, was a typical, gloomy, overcast day
in Brittany. Early that morning when the train arrived
at Brest, I climbed down from my upper *couchette*, where,
in full uniform and heavy overcoat, I had spent a restless
night. Placing undue confidence in my luck, I had given
my pillow and blanket to one of Chaplain Goldberg's men
on the station platform in Paris. Goldberg had under his
wing a group of sight-seeing transport sailors, and he was

in quest of a blanket. Even with expert pantomime he was unable to make the porter understand. He lowered his head on the backs of his hands as though falling asleep and then drew up over his ears a blanket that was not there. All to no avail. I gave him mine. The porter had issued his last one. I slept in my clothes on the flat, hard *couchette;* and the night was cold.

I registered for a room at Brest's Hotel Continental and reported to Vice Admiral Henry B. Wilson, Commander of Naval Forces in France, "for such duty as may be assigned you." His office was on the Place du Champ de Bataille. At Scapa Flow Rear Admiral Hugh Rodman had told me about "Tug" Wilson, predicting, in his peculiar way, that I would find it interesting "sky-piloting up and down the coast of France" in the latter's command. Being prepared to brave it through with the brusque "Tug," I actually enjoyed my first interview with him.

Admiral Wilson was pacing his office when they announced me and he puffed on a long cigar. Greeting me cordially, he offered me a chair and something to smoke. But he quickly opened fire; he fairly bellowed, "Do you get along with the Y.M.C.A.?" I replied there was every reason to coöperate. "Your predecessor fought with them. I sent him home. I want you to get along with them. If they get tough, let me know. They're doing good work. You'll be base chaplain here. If you want to go to sea, the flag secretary will arrange. If the men don't go to church at first, don't get sore. Give 'em time to know you."

A voice came from the adjoining room. Commander John Halligan, the chief of staff, shouted, "They'll go to Mass, Father, I'll be there myself." His timely word of cheer reassured me. Years later, when John Halligan was an admiral, I reminded him of that helpful speech.

Admiral Wilson had a capable staff. In the official family was Commander Frank Taylor Evans, a replica of his famous father, Admiral "Fighting Bob." He and the young flag lieutenant, Mahlon "Tip" Tisdale were always ready to help me, especially in my work with the general courtmartial prisoners who, for a time, were locked in a medieval dungeon. Being close to the admiral they helped me convince the stern "Tug" it was better to place the men in our own brig.

Here was a job to be designed and built. Not having "taken over" from my predecessor, how to begin was a puzzle.

The thousands of sailors that crowded the streets of the town and manned the ships of the Breton patrol must know, I thought, where to find the chaplain. Being the only one on duty at the base, I asked Captain Henry Hough, the district commandant, for an office. But my varied duties—visiting three hospitals daily and boarding ships to interview the men—nullified the need of a desk except as a place to pick up messages. Mine became a roving commission.

The admiral heartily approved my going to sea. He said, "That's where a chaplain is needed—in the ships. Let the y and the k. of c. look after the men when they're ashore." Ministering to the sick and dying in the hospital, however, became my major task. During the influenza epidemic I rode in a motor-cycle sidecar on calls to the army camp at Pontenezen and to hospitals farther in the country. Nearly every afternoon I marched in the funeral cortege through the streets of Brest to the cemetery. The French bystanders stood reverently as we passed; the women making the sign of the cross while the men, with heads bowed, doffed their hats. During that fateful period, burials often took place at midnight, lest the French lose heart.

Whenever a lull came I sought a chance to spend a week in the convoys. My especial pet was the coal-burning destroyer, *Smith*. Her commanding officer, Lieutenant Commander "Jakie" Klein, came to me one evening in the officers' mess and invited me to "take a ride." That was the beginning of a series of sea trips which endeared me to the Navy's better half—her ships and her seagoing men. Joining our Kelly-pool game, Klein drew me aside and whispered that his motor dory would be at the landing at three the following afternoon. With orders for temporary duty in the *Smith* and my heart dancing in my breast, the next day I hopped the little boat and "put-putted" across the bay. On the welldeck of the destroyer I found the tall, blue-eyed John Heffernan, the gunnery officer, and Richard L. Connolly, the chief engineer. They have since gone the long, hard way to important commands in the Fleet.

Like the other officers, I dressed in leather boots and sheepskin coat, worn over my service blues. For want of space, I slept on a cot in the wardroom, removing only my boots. Klein slept close by on a leather transom. Above his head, within a few inches of his quick ears, hung the brass opening of a voice tube. The officer of the deck on the bridge at the other end of it had no respect for the skipper's need for sleep, whenever important news turned up in the night watches.

Our mission, on that first sortie, was to escort the faster

transports beyond the submarine zone and then to pick up another fast convoy heading for France. Other times we convoyed slower ships.

Our mission one day was to contact a convoy of cargo ships off the coast of England. At five-thirty in the morning I heard the officer of the deck calling to Klein.

"Wardroom. . . ." It startled me.

Klein, half awake, called back, "This is the captain."

"We have made contact with the convoy. I just saw a big splash. It may be a torpedo hit." He spoke each word distinctly.

"I'll be right up," said Klein. Then to me, with a lusty punch on my ribs, "Come on, padré, and see some action."

I pulled on my boots and followed him through the narrow passageway to the welldeck and up the ladder to the bridge. It was misty but we could see a merchantman sinking fast by the bow. The officer in command of the American flotilla ordered his destroyers to lay down a depth-charge barrage. Speeding in a wide circle, we raced like bloodhounds, dropping cans of TNT in the area where we hoped the U-boat was prowling.

While this breathtaking show was on, some one noticed a British destroyer lower its observation balloon. It was a strange maneuver at such a critical moment. A bluejacket on the welldeck thought he knew. I heard him shout. "The limey wasn't in the basket. . . . 'E's below 'aving 'is dish of tea."

The *Smith* belonged to the legendary "dungaree navy." Once she reached the wide savannahs of the deep, the "black gang" of the little coal-burner really became black. Like most destroyer crews, her men were cheerful and hard-working—all-round fine shipmates. It was inspiring to chat with them when they came to topside for a "blow."

One day at sea they gave me a puppy, one of a pair a sailor carried back after a liberty in Brest. A coal passer yelled down the after hatch, "Hey, below, hand up the chaplain's dog." In a grimy fist a tiny pup appeared—black as pitch and just as sticky. With strong feelings of pride, I carried him to the wardroom and sought advice on a suitable name to give him. All agreed we should call him "Smitty."

When I returned to my room in the tender *Prometheus* at the end of that trip, I washed the little beast and discovered he was a quasi-Dalmatian. He became a favorite of the crew. For a month or more, for his own good, Smitty was denied shore liberty. But one day he made his debut on the boulevard. I fastened on his new collar and carried him down the ladder to the boat. He seemed to like that, being still in his favorite element. But when we reached the boulevard and for the first time he saw little children who, he probably thought, were inhabitants of a strange world, he bolted and ran like the wind. Smitty had lived only with grown-ups. He had never seen anything so small or so lively as little boys. We gave chase and caught him only because his little legs were unaccustomed to long runs. That was Smitty's first and only liberty. He remained thereafter a dog of the sea.

With the skipper of the *Smith*, when at sea, I often stood on the hurricane deck hoping something might turn up. Occasionally Klein, while holding in his hand an "allo"—a message telling of the places where subs had been sighted—would say, "How's to say a prayer, padré, for a chance to get one of those subs?" Rummaging through an old scrapbook recently, I ran across a message which probably was the one Klein held in his hand. The date was April 3, 1918. The origin, the armed yacht *Ravenska*, sent via Landsend. "Area 14 to all allied ships. Passed wake of submarine fifty 05 North four fifty two West. Dropped depth charges. Destroyer informed and dropping depth charges . . ." But Klein was too far from the scene to be interested.

Memorial Day, 1918, might have been devoted to sports had not President Woodrow Wilson proclaimed it a day of prayer. They put me in charge of the naval proceedings. To make the program full and comprehensive, I planned having a military field Mass in the morning, services under Protestant auspices at Ker Faustras Cemetery in the afternoon, and to have the admiral give an inspirational talk at the big Y hut in the evening.

I chose for our military Mass the large courtyard of the old barracks built in Napoleon's day, known as Caserne Faustras. We called the place "Carola Barracks." Against the building at the end of the quadrangle, we placed two French trucks side by side, and built a deck over them. We improvised an altar, borrowing vestments and fixtures from a nearby church, and formed a dossal by rigging alternate French and American flags. I invited the French chaplain of the cruiser *Jeanne d'Arc* to be celebrant, Father Boisvert of the A.E.F. to be acolyte, and Father Jim Sherry, a Bostonian, also of the Army, to preach the sermon. I acted as a sort of master of ceremonies and opened the services with an announcement relating to the plan of the day.

As Father Sherry mounted the platform to preach, I recalled my fears of the evening before when he came to my apartment pretending his throat was so sore he could not speak aloud. For nearly an hour he had tortured me, whispering that I had better get a sermon ready, insisting that he was completely *hors de combat*. When I was on the point of politely inviting him to leave and allow me time to whip up a few ideas, he bellowed in a loud baritone, "Take it easy, Mac—I'll be there." He preached a splendid sermon to that important congregation and he won a "well done," from Admiral Wilson. Half of the congregation were French sailors; they and the American bluejackets formed a square, and in the corner stood hundreds of officers among whom were generals and admirals, American and British and French. The day was a solemn one. I little thought then that six years later I would again stand in Ker Faustras Cemetery and read the same prayers on Memorial Day. I was then serving in destroyer division #39; we were en route from Turkish waters to New York.

We might have had a photographic souvenir of the 1918 Ker Faustras service had not Irvin Cobb, who sat in the second row of the speakers' stand, absent-mindedly displayed his smoking cigar. It added no solemnity. The admiral, when he saw it the next day, gave fiery orders to destroy the negative.

I enjoyed many talks with Irvin Cobb while he was in Brest but we did not always see eye to eye on the German invasion of Belgium. We had viewed Belgium's 1914 from quite different angles; he had been the guest of Prussian officers; I had lived with the sufferers.

One morning, in a little church near the landing, I had the honor of giving Major Philip Torrey, U.S. Marine Corps, his first Holy Communion. As he knelt alone at the altar rail, just before I came down from the altar with the Sacred Host, a navy band, marching with a battalion of sailors, played "Over There." My friend Phil, who is now a major general in the marine corps, left that day for the front line where he inspected for three weeks under fire. It was part of his training as a future regimental commander. On his return to Brest he had to wait a few days before sailing to join his regiment at Quantico, Virginia. He came to my apartment directly from the train, but he looked sadly depressed. That evening he told me what was troubling his soul.

"Padré, I'm a quitter. I'm ashamed to tell you what happened the other night. We were in a dugout and the Germans were raining high explosives on us. We played cards, trying to be calm. When the time came to turn in I didn't have the nerve to kneel when I said my prayers. I thought the others might think I was afraid of the shelling. I said my night prayers lying flat on the ground under my blanket. I guess I haven't got what it takes." Phil seemed relieved when I told him I thought Almighty God did not always require us to kneel when reverently addressing Him.

In the naval officers mess at luncheon one day I met a young Y.M.C.A. Secretary, Alfred de Groot Vogler, from Pennsylvania. He, a Presbyterian minister, wondered how he might join the navy chaplain corps. He had the personality and "pepper" the Navy expects of a chaplain. Feeling a bit presumptuous, I gave him, nevertheless, a letter to the Secretary of the Navy and another to father, recommending him enthusiastically. For many years Al and I have been together in the Fleet. Last winter he invited me to celebrate a Solemn High Midnight Mass on board his ship, the carrier, *Enterprise*, in the navy yard at Bremerton, Washington. Captain Charles A. Pownall then commanded that splendid ship. Three thousand officers and men assisted at Mass on the hangar deck.

Thoughts of Brest bring to mind the many happy hours I spent with Dr. Thomas Healy of Newburyport, Massachusetts. Dr. Tom had charge of the X-ray Department of one of the naval hospitals and has since made a distinguished record in Boston. He has honored me every Christmas by sending me a fine book about the sea.

Sunday mornings, during the early part of my year in Brest, I celebrated early Mass at the air station in a tent on the bare ground. I then took a boat and offered a second Mass on board the tender *Prometheus*. Usually there were four or five destroyers alongside, and there were many confessions to be heard before Mass. After the second Mass, I again went ashore and held a general service in Carola Barracks. This service was requested by Admiral Wilson. He thought it proper that I, being the only navy chaplain at the base, should minister to all hands. He and his staff always attended and there were several Red Cross nurses and other civilian war workers present. The famous Carola orchestra played for the singing. I held the first general service dressed in my service blues. The Admiral came to me at the close and asked whether the Church would object to my wearing something more ecclesiastical. To please him I thereafter wore a cassock, surplice and stole.

One morning, while I was preaching at the general service, I became uncomfortably distracted by a man who seemed dressed in the uniform of a welfare secretary. He stared at me and I wondered, with my nerves on edge from fatigue, whether he was "on my team" or only there to criticise. After the service, I discovered it was Witwer, a war correspondent. I invited him to breakfast at the officers' mess and we soon became fast friends. He told me that he intended to write a book about Catholic war chaplains. He had met so many of them. He knew Father John Brady of the Navy, having crawled with him on hands and knees through the wheat field when the marines fought at Belleau Woods. Witwer had heard of my experience in the *Florence H.* disaster and he said he intended putting that story in his book. He stayed with me in my apartment on Rue Emile Zola and we had enjoyable talks. He regaled me with yarns about Jack London whom he knew intimately during the more hungry years of London's career. I last saw Witwer as he boarded a train for Marseilles. He intended spending several weeks with the forces under the command of Admiral Niblack in the Mediterranean. As later he succumbed to influenza en route to the United States, his book on the Catholic war padres, I fear, was never written.

I found it none too easy to preach at the general service. I still quiver over the importance and the responsibility involved in preaching to a mixed congregation. During the greater part of my stay in Brest, I celebrated my second Mass in the spacious Y.M.C.A. hut. The secretaries of the Y were as kind and helpful to me then as they since have been in many parts of the world. The Knights of Columbus conducted a service men's club in Brest. Bill O'Neil was in charge. But it lacked the space required for large groups. I remained throughout at the Y.

Several army chaplains came through Brest. At Pontenezen I met Chaplain Mitty, now Archbishop of San Francisco. One evening on Rue de Siam, I hailed two new arrivals—one was a chaplain. They were Father Walsh and Don Miller of Notre Dame University. I invited them to dine with me at our mess. The tall, scholarly Father Walsh was a first lieutenant, but young Don Miller was a captain. I joked about this at dinner, for the chaplain was years older than Miller. This apparently had been laughed over before and they told me of their first military clash, when Father Walsh reported for duty at a cantonment. Miller was officer of the day and he knew that the former Vice President of Notre Dame had orders to his outfit. He also recalled the many times Father Walsh had denied him the privilege of leaving the campus to visit friends in South Bend. Here is the story:

The tall priest entered the tent and finding Miller sitting at a desk, exclaimed:

"Well, well, Miller. Fancy finding you here!"

Miller stiffly replied, "Captain Miller to you, Chaplain."

"Very well," said the priest, a bit hurt. "Captain Miller, I've come for a pass. I have things to do in town . . ."

Miller glared at him with feigned annoyance. "Not granted, Sir." He kept his face rigid.

"But, Miller, I . . ."

"Captain Miller, if you please."

Don Miller finally relented and wrote out a pass for the bewildered priest. After the chaplain left the tent, Miller issued a duplicate pass and mailed it to the university where, if I remember correctly, it was framed and hung on the wall of the vice president's office. Miller laughingly said that he simply could not resist the temptation to "get square." They were a happy pair and I knew that the soldiers of their machine gun battalion were more than lucky to have them as "buddies." Don Miller later became mayor of Cleveland, Ohio.

One of the most interesting chaplains I met at Brest was Father Mario "Jerry" Garriga, of the Texas division, now the Bishop of Corpus Christi. When I last saw him, in the summer of 1918, he was a barrel-chested campaigner in boots and spurs who had lately come from the Mexican border. He wasted no sympathy on the "rooky" priests who had joined up in 1917. Father Jerry was a seasoned veteran and he didn't care who knew it. His general had honored him with orders to join a group of line officers sent to France a month ahead of the Texas division in order to arrange for their arrival and prepare a suitable reception for them. I discovered years later that my old school friend, Lucien Coppinger, was also in the Texas division, an aide-de-camp on the general's staff.

One day Father Garriga announced that his "kids," as he called them, were to arrive on the morrow and that he probably would not join me until late in the evening. I went to his room at the hotel and waited. He returned about dinner time. The day had been humid and warm; he was covered with dust and his uniform was soaked with perspiration. He threw himself on the bed and groaned. "I'm dog tired. I had to walk all the way back from

Pontenezen. But I'm not going to worry about my kids any more. When I arrived at the camp I was thirsty and asked one of the sergeants for a swig from his canteen. The lad hesitated, said it was warm as soup and reckoned I wouldn't like it. I insisted and—guess what it was?—champagne! He had stepped out of line and bought a bottle at an *estaminet* near the landing. He said some of the men had beer in their canteens, others sauterne. Imagine that, fresh from Texas! Those kids know their way around!"

I spent an enjoyable month with the future Bishop of Corpus Christi, and I hope some day to pay His Excellency my respects and to remind him of our war days in Brittany.

Admiral Wilson put me in charge of a fund we had raised by giving shows in the local opera house. He directed me to spend the money buying articles of comfort for the French and American wounded. One day I was passing out handkerchiefs and safety razors to a group of wounded marines. When I was about to hand a razor to a marine whose legs had been amputated, the lad declined, saying he had no use for it. He was only sixteen. Across from him I noticed a marine swaying back and forth on his bed, moaning a little. He too had lost a leg. While chatting with him I asked whether he had met my friend, Father John Brady. The lad smiled. "Do I know him! He's the swellest guy in the world. I'm a Jew but it didn't make any difference." Swaying back and forth, holding his thigh he kept saying, "He's the best guy I know." The others in the ward heard him. One shouted. "Who ya talkin' about?"

"Father Brady."

They asked me if I knew him. Then, "Yeah, he's a swell guy. Give 'm our best when yuh see 'm."

I told this yarn to Father John when he was fleet chaplain in 1933. Father Brady, though modestly opposed to publicity, was a true hero in the estimation of the Devil Dogs of Belleau Woods. The marines were also loud in their praise of the late Father Darche and Chaplains Mac-Nair and Park who are now retired on account of physical disability. These navy chaplains were decorated by the high command of the American and French armies for conspicuous bravery under fire.

One day, when the Assistant Secretary of the Navy, Franklin Delano Roosevelt, came to Brest, the members of the naval officers mess gave him a reception. He made a circuit of the room, meeting the officers. I recall how he looked that day: a tall figure, vigorous, athletic and cheerful. His large, clear blue eyes captivated me and made me feel quite at ease.

When I was introduced, he grasped my hand and said, "Father Maguire, you have a big job. I want you to know that I am deeply interested in your work with the men. Good luck."

Years later, when I read in the papers that President Roosevelt, in his capacity as Commander-in-Chief of the Army and Navy, conducted divine services one Sunday at sea, I remembered that moment in Brest which meant so much to me, when I was young and needed a helping hand.

CHAPTER 11

The Florence H.

THE young skipper of the armed yacht, *Christabel*, Lieutenant Commander Millington B. McComb, sat next to me one day in April at luncheon in the naval officers' mess; and he invited me to join him on a coastal convoy trip. The idea had an especial appeal for I anticipated action; a German submarine had lately sunk four of our ships. At that time, convoys were run at night. The system now called for daylight steaming. I had a premonition that something might turn up.

I boarded the *Christabel* in the early afternoon and found McComb preparing to board the destroyer *Whipple* for a conference. He suggested that I accompany him. The *Whipple* was an old coal-burner and rather tiny. Weather-beaten skippers of the merchant marine packed the little wardroom. These tough sea dogs seemed bored with the idea of taking orders from young Lieutenant Commander "Jock" Abbott, senior officer of the convoy. But Abbott laid down the law. He told them what speed they must maintain and how important it was to hold the ships in position. He did most of the talking, and he wasted no words.

At dawn the next morning, April 17th, we all got under way, steamed out the narrow channel to sea and set a course to the southward, about five miles off the coast. There were about fifteen merchantmen, five armed yachts and the two destroyers, *Whipple* and *Stewart*. All hands on topside constantly scanned the waters for a sight of the enemy's periscope. Nothing unusual happened, but Captain Abbott's *Whipple* raced about all day like a shepherd dog to keep the ships in position. We arrived at Quiberon Bay at eleven that night and dropped anchor behind the nets. A few of us joined McComb in the wardroom for a cup of coffee. We were about to turn in when we heard a terrific explosion; and a brilliant flash of light illuminated the whole bay. It was the *Florence H.*, the largest ship in the convoy. I remembered her fantastic camouflage in black and gray. We rushed to the rail and beheld the horror of a great ship ablaze. McComb ordered a boat lowered. I asked permission to go along to help in the rescue of survivors. The skipper nodded assent and I leaped down the hatch to get my sheepskin coat. I also took along the Blessed Sacrament and the Holy Oils. In a jiffy I followed the ship's medico, Dr. G. E. Cram, into the motor whaleboat. We set out on our grim mission.

The survivors were terribly burned. Some died in the destroyer *Stewart* on the way to Brest. I administered the last rites to several men. One of the *Florence H.* men came to me early the following morning and said he had failed to find his brother. He had carefully searched the compartment where the seriously injured lay. I told him there were still three survivors left on board the yacht *Sultana*. Dr. Cram and I had made a tour of the bay and attended the wounded. It was a thrill to learn the next day that the sailor's brother was one of the three on board the yacht. Ambulances were at the Brest landing when we arrived the morning of the 18th. A newly renovated ward was in readiness in Naval Hospital No. 5. Doctors, nurses and corpsmen were on the alert and prepared for their delicate mission.

There was one survivor in the ward whom the others despised. Whether justified or not, they believed this man had set a time bomb which destroyed the *Florence H*. They said he was the first to leave the ship. He also managed to be the first to leave the hospital; only his hands were burned. Rumors were heard a few days later to the effect that the French had found the unpopular sailor prowling about the submarine base and that they had shot him for espionage.

The Navy Board of Awards recommended that we *Christabel* people be given the Navy Cross "for extraordinary heroism." I received my Cross in the spring of 1920 on the quarterdeck of the U.S.S. *Idaho* in the presence of the ship's company. The admiral in command of the Battleship Division 3, came over and read the citation and pinned the Cross on my blouse.

I visited my brother Walter at Portland, Oregon, during the Christmas holidays. My name appeared in the papers along with a story of the *Florence H*. One evening in the lobby of the Multnomah Hotel, a woman came up to me and said that her only son had been killed in the *Florence H*. She wondered whether her boy had been at his post at the time of the explosion and added that he had the rating of quartermaster. I told her that I believed he was on the bridge when it all happened. Only members of the engineers force were saved. It pleased the good woman to be told her boy had died at his post.

Six years later, when I served on the staff of the commander aircraft squadrons in the Pacific Fleet, McComb and I again were shipmates. He had become an aviator and now commanded an observation squadron. His wingmates held him in high repute. They marvelled at his daring and uncanny skill in finding the air field in foul weather. I last saw "Mac" in 1925 when he commanded the air station at Pearl Harbor, Hawaii. I had lunch with him in his quarters. The poor fellow was killed that year in a crash over the sea near Honolulu.

I made a second cruise in the yachts of the Breton patrol. I went as the "guest chaplain" of Howard H. J. Benson who now commands the new super-dreadnaught, the U.S.S. *Washington*. Howard then commanded the *Carola*. I still recall our being assigned to patrol duty alone off the coast in search of a mine-laying U-boat. We all knew that the sub's speed even when submerged exceeded the *Carola's*. But the sub decided that day not to fight.

CHAPTER 12

A Son of Saint Francis

ONE day, in the summer of 1918, I met an army chaplain on Rue de Siam in Brest. The street was crowded with service people—soldiers, sailors, nurses, American telephone operators and men of the armed forces of France, the British Isles and Portugal. As always on discovering a cross on an officer's blouse, I introduced myself. The army chaplain was Father Juniper Doolin, a Franciscan from California. I took him to our mess for dinner. He had arrived that morning in a transport and was on his way to the front as a "casual" with orders to remain at Brest until official word came assigning him to a regiment in training for the front line.

During that trying period, I was giving more of my time to the soldiers than to the men in blue. I was delighted to have Father Juniper's help in the army hospitals. The influenza epidemic was raging and I usually felt pretty well done in by midnight when I stood in the flare of the gas torches at Pontenezen Cemetery to read, in the rain, funeral services over men buried there in long, deep, narrow trenches. Such mass burials were held at night lest the French civilians suffer further strain on their tortured nerves. They were not told of these horrors. The Army had no base chaplain at Brest. Admiral Wilson disapproved of my strenuous routine although he understood my responsibility as a priest under the tragic circumstances. He, consequently, ordered me to proceed to Chaumont and to request of the chief of chaplains of the Army that a priest be ordered to Brest to lend a hand. My interesting mission which had all the earmarks of a vacation, was a success. The Army ordered Father Joseph Kangley, a veteran of the regular Army, to Brest.

Father Juniper was keen on this chance to get back to work. He was as smart and bright as a new dollar and his ready smile revealed a knack for discovering the humorous side even in tragic times.

We visited the hospitals together. One afternoon, I found him attending the dying in a ward filled with German prisoners. He spoke German fluently. He also handled French well enough to crack jokes with the waiters. I remarked what a fine linguist the Army had acquired. He was glad, he said, to brush up on his German and French but had misgivings about his Chinese. I misinterpreted his smile.

We were walking on crowded Rue de Siam a few days later when he suddenly left me and disappeared in the crowd. When I found him, he was talking fluent Chinese with a coolie, a member of a stevedore battalion from Indo-China. People gathered around amazed. A sailor asked me, "What's he doin'—bawlin' out the chink?" The coolie bowed excitedly and there were tears of joy streaming from his almond eyes. My friend Doolin could not have chosen a more favorable spot to dramatize his working knowledge of the coolie's mother tongue. He had not told me of his fourteen years of missionary labor in fields afar. "*Voilà*, Mac, you thought I was kidding." The sailors nearby thought I had lost a bet.

The day finally came when Father Juniper waved a paper before my eyes. "Here it is—my orders. I'm leaving for the front."

After the war, two years later, I went to the old mission of Santa Barbara to make a private retreat. Two friends from the Pacific Fleet, Father Tom Burke, now a pastor in Chicago, and Lieutenant Francis W. Benson, went with me. I immediately inquired about Father Juniper and they told me he was critically ill following a stroke. He was in some distant hospital; the friars expected to be told at any moment of Juniper's death. A few days after my return to the *Idaho*, I was detached and for twenty years my duties took me far from home, even around the world. But I never forgot the jolly friar of the Brest days. He was so like St. Francis of Assisi.

In the fall of 1938, I was again in the Fleet, this time as force chaplain of the scouting force, serving in the heavy cruiser *Indianapolis*. With Father Frank McManus, chaplain of the U.S.S. *Maryland*, I again knocked on the oaken door of the old mission. We had come to make a retreat. Arriving after dusk, I was too weary to join the friars in their recreation room and I turned in early.

After Mass the next day, I went to a small chapel to read my breviary. For several minutes the place was serenely quiet. Then I heard a strange sound, as if something heavy were being dragged down the corridor. Someone opened the chapel door and I turned my head to express with a frown a faint disapproval of the noise. I thought my eyes had tricked me. I actually saw Father Juniper. It was his poor crippled leg he was dragging—a souvenir of the stroke that had afflicted him eighteen years before. His hair was snow white but his face had not changed much; there were new lines, but the smile I had known was there. His friar's habit was becoming but I could still see the ghost of an army blouse and the swank of his Sam Browne belt.

He came over where I was kneeling and whispered, "I had to say hello—they told me you were here." The only words that came were, "Impossible. I've been praying for the repose of your soul for eighteen years." That smile again. Juniper was not dead! Juniper will never die! He may be detached some day from his earthly duties but he will never die.

Before leaving the old mission, Father Juniper invited me to address the students of the college. I gave them a word-picture of their venerable spiritual director, as I had once known him—a warrior of God under the command of the Prince of Peace.

CHAPTER 13

I Rejoin the Fleet

On a rainy morning in Brest I met Father Gleeson, the fleet chaplain, in the recreation room of the Knights of Columbus. He was nearly fifty then and in the pink of health. Under his rain-soaked "brass hat" his sunny smile put me quickly at ease. It was his custom to know everyone's given name. Some of my friends thought it was a part of his "system." He jovially grasped my hand, "Good morning, William, me b'y. I've been hearing of the splendid work you've been doing over here." The good padre, I think, "wrote the book" on Blarney technique. "They tell me you're leaving soon. Where would you like to go?" I told him I looked forward to battleship duty in the Fleet. "I'll keep that in mind, William." Father Gleeson meant what he said.

In the destroyer tender, *Prometheus*, I made the homeward bound trip to New York. The blue pennant with white stars at the main truck, which signified we had been overseas for more than a year, was at least thirty feet long. We all got a piece of it.

On a cold day in February, a little after dark, we dropped anchor in New York Bay. I was standing next to Captain Frank Lyons on the welldeck discussing arrangements for a ship's ball we were planning to hold at the old Waldorf-Astoria. Our conversation was sharply interrupted when a voice came out of the darkness hailing us. In a moment we made out the lines of a tug boat and then the words, "Lehigh Valley R.R." Through a megaphone a man yelled again, "Is Father Maguire on board?" The bosun's mate replied for us. Then, "His father, Mr. J. F. Maguire, is here and wants to speak to him." I was almost breathless. I took the megaphone and called a greeting to father. He, too, was moved; his voice faltered but he managed to say, "Welcome home, Will. Can you join me? We'll take along any who want to go ashore . . ." I quickly asked the captain's permission to leave the ship and suggested that I take along the members of the ball committee. The word was passed to them; I rushed to my room, shaking with anticipation, and packed. Never had I been so completely moved. It was like a surprise twist in a play.

We climbed over the *Prometheus'* side and down the wobbly Jacob's ladder and then leaped aboard the tug. Gaiety and tears marked this meeting. Our *Prometheus* shipmates gave us an envious wave of farewell as the tug veered toward the lighted skyline of our beloved New York. I put the committee up at the Catholic Club on Central Park South and told them to shake a leg the next day and invite to the ship's ball telephone operators, Y.W.C.A. girls, sales-girls from Wanamaker's and yeomanettes from the Navy Yard. In mid-Atlantic we had booked the ballroom by radio for the following night. My "gang" did nobly, and their shipmates were elated. The golden ballroom of the old Waldorf-Astoria had never seen a gayer jamboree. Father, of course, attended, and my sister Anita came down from Bethlehem.

A few hours "after the ball was over" the ship got under way for Norfolk. The captain granted ten days' leave and I set a course for my home in Bethlehem, Pennsylvania, where father had his main office.

The Reverend Matthew Gleeson had not forgotten me. After five exciting days of parties and lectures, a dispatch came ordering me detached and to report to the U.S.S. *Idaho*, a new battleship fitting out in a Camden, N. J., shipyard. The *Idaho* was being built by the New York Shipbuilding Company. Our enlisted men were temporarily billeted in the Navy Yard on the opposite shore of the Delaware. The commanding officer, Captain Carl T. Vogelgesang, had asked his old friend, the fleet chaplain, to recommend a Catholic chaplain for his latest ship command. I was too junior even to hope for such an assignment.

During my short stay in Philadelphia I had the privilege of meeting Agnes Repplier in her home. The distinguished essayist had that day received a letter from Woodrow Wilson asking her opinion of the proposal to exhume the buried heroes of the A.E.F. and to return them to the homeland. Her arguments pro and con were masterful. Miss Repplier requested that I help her decide. I voted to permit our dead to remain in France.

Having the *Idaho* sailors in camp at the Navy Yard gave me a good chance to become acquainted with them. I passed around a questionnaire which would record each man's religion and his special talents for Happy Hours and athletics. We had several clever lads in the crew; many of them had been on the professional stage. Several months later they proved how good they were when our show "Tea for Two" ran a week in a Los Angeles theatre.

On March 24, 1919, we all embarked in tugs and crossed the Delaware to take possession of our $30,000,000 "yacht." Captain Vogelgesang, in the presence of his ship's company, read his orders and ran up his commission pennant. We soon got under way for New York where we took on stores and ammunition in preparation for the shake-down cruise in the Caribbean.

En route to Guantanamo Bay it was apparent that the wardroom officers did not really know one another. The senior officers had spent most of their time in the Camden ship yard. We junior people of the "Fourth Ward" had been occupied with the men in the *Idaho* camp across the river. The atmosphere in the wardroom was a bit chilly. But on the afternoon we dropped the hook in Guantanamo Bay a time-honored way to rectify that deficiency was revived. Most of the members of the mess went up to the "Oasis" in the small town of Caimanera. Thoroughly acquainted, the officers returned, singing all the way to the ship, and sustaining their high spirits throughout dinner. This extraordinary frivolity must have tested the patience of Commander Ralston Holmes, our popular executive officer. At the highest peak of our fun, when the paymaster was leading in song, intoning something like,

> Let's have another drink to quench our thirst,
> The States go dry on July first. . . .

Captain Vogelgesang appeared. He gave the mess a frigid stare. Our first impulse was to slide under the table. The captain smiled. "Gentlemen," he said, "I'm glad to see that the ice is broken. This'll be a happy ship." He quickly disappeared and we, contrary to navy custom, gave the "Old Man" a hearty cheer.

There were two Brazilian naval officers attached to the *Idaho*, Lieutenant Hugo "Jimmy" Pontes and Mario "Bill" Coutinho; they were well liked by all hands. "Jimmy" was a most versatile fellow. He spoke fluently six languages: English (perfectly), French, German, Italian, Spanish, and of course his mother tongue, Portuguese. He was blessed with a splendid voice and often sang for the crew at Happy Hours. I went to his room one day at sea; Jimmy was modeling in clay. I asked him, "When did you meet Pauline Frederick?" Jimmy rose and said, "Thank you. Does it really look like her?" When it was finished he had a model struck from it and he gave it to the movie lady who had inspired his mood. He drew cartoons for the ship's paper, *The Yarn*. One morning at San Pedro, California, Jimmy entered the wardroom while we were at breakfast. He carried a huge loving cup which he said he had won in a dancing contest at "Ship's Café" in Venice. I believe he said Buster Keaton and his partner were runners up. But Jimmy Pontes did not allow his wide versatility to prevent his excelling in his profession. He was the best gunnery spotter in the Pacific Fleet. Bill and Jimmy spent two years with us on the *Idaho*.

The high light of the shake-down cruise was our Easter service in Guantanamo Bay. Captain Vogelgesang sent for me on Holy Thursday and asked me to read the proclamation he intended to post on the ship's bulletin board. Here it is:

SPECIAL NOTICE
EASTER SUNDAY

1. The Commanding Officer desires to call especial attention of the officers and crew of the *Idaho* to the fact that next Sunday, April 20th, will be Easter Sunday.

2. This is one of the days of the greatest importance in the church calendar and on which all who profess to be Christians, whatever their denomination, should attend Divine Services.

3. Your Commanding Officer, therefore, expresses the hope that all who are not on particular duty concerned with the running of the ship during the forenoon watch next Sunday morning will respond to the church call. The Services will be held on the quarterdeck, weather permitting, and there will be room for all.

4. If you have been brought up to go to church, you will, by attendance, fulfill a Christian obligation; if you have never gone to church, this will be a good chance to begin. Of one thing we may be sure—it will not hurt anyone, and it will be good for us all.

5. Let us play the game in the spiritual as well as the material sense.

6. Your Commanding Officer looks for an extraordinary attendance at Divine Worship on this, which will be, in effect, our first Sunday together.

On Saturday at luncheon Commander Holmes asked the officers who had sung in the Naval Academy choir to raise their hands. "That's fine," he said. "There'll be a choir rehearsal in the wardroom at one o'clock. Padre, break out the hymn books." The officers' choir sang even better at the Easter service.

At the close of the "All Hands" service, just prior to Mass, Captain Vogelgesang rose and commended the ship's company for their response to his appeal for recognition of the importance of Easter Sunday. He said there were at least nine hundred on the quarterdeck, the largest sea-going congregation he had ever seen. It made us very proud of the *Idaho* and her skipper.

On our arrival in New York, the mess invited a few friends for luncheon. The young ladies of the party, who were members of the chorus of Shanley's floor show, became especially interested in Lieutenant "Bill" Coutinho, the Brazilian. They smothered him with questions. His accent amused them. But "Bill," now in the limelight, put on an act. Many of his replies were profane. As he scrambled his faulty English and occasionally seasoned his chatter with expressions that even a sailor's parrot might eschew he kept a straight face. One of the girls asked Bill, "I say, Lieutenant, who's teaching you English?" The wag from Rio pointed at me. "Dat's him, ober dare, de padre."

I requested ten days' leave and visited my home in Bethlehem. It was an attractive place which father had recently bought. There was a tennis court and a lovely flower garden. From the porch one got a view of the Lehigh River and the fine farms in the valley. One afternoon while Anita and I were sitting on the porch discussing a name for a ship's paper I proposed to launch for the *Idaho*, we hit upon the word "yarn." *The Yarn* for twenty years has broken the Fleet news to the men of the good ship, *Idaho*. That day a telegram from New York informed me that the ship had sailing orders to convey the President of Brazil, Epitacio Pessoa, his family and retinue, to Rio de Janeiro. I caught the 7:15 in the morning.

CHAPTER 14

The Army Nurse

ONE evening during the period when the ship's company had waited in the Philadelphia Navy Yard for orders to cross the Delaware and take possession of the new battleship *Idaho*, I visited St. Patrick's rectory near Rittenhouse Square. The young curates and a few clerical friends were lounging in the recreation room when they began to question me about my war experiences. They were especially interested in the hospitals at Brest and the work of the doctors and nurses, for an important unit on duty there was made up of Philadelphians, many of whom they knew. I told them of the army nurse.

In our group there was a visitor from the South, an old priest who was on his annual visit to the pastor. He sat near a window, puffing on his aged pipe and uttering not a word; he seemed content to listen to us younger men.

"It may interest you to know," I said, "that the most heroic person I met in those days was a little red-headed nurse from North Carolina."

The old priest turned from the window where he had been gazing upon the lighted street below. What I had said startled him.

I continued, and told them of the frail nurse who, with many other American girls, had sailed from Halifax and

97

arrived in the dark at Glasgow, Scotland. Without pause and still in darkness, the nurses embarked for a Channel port and took a train for Paris, arriving again, after dark. That seemed to be the most annoying feature of their adventure—always arriving in the dark and seeing nothing of interest. At night in Paris they boarded a train for Brest, and they arrived long after sunset. They immediately climbed, forty of them, onto an army truck and bounded over the cobble road to the hospital at Pontenezen. No sooner had they begun to relax than a doctor came and called for volunteers to report immediately to a ward where soldiers were critically ill with spinal meningitis.

The nurses were tired and discouraged. Some had developed colds. One especially was quite ill—little Miss Shannon from Raleigh, North Carolina. Against the advice of several of her companions she was the first to volunteer her services; she went at once to the ward tent and put on mask and gloves for a merciful tour of duty in that perilous place of contagion.

Summoned the next day to attend the dying in the ward, I met Miss Shannon. I shall never forget how well she had prepared the scene for me.

"Good morning, Father, we're ready for you." Her weary, freckled face attempted a smile. She helped me into a gown and a mask. She showed me a list of all the Catholic men who were in danger of death, and she led the way to each bed and introduced me cheerfully to each of the patients who were especially in need. Her devotion to those poor fellows was impressive, but when she knelt beside their bed while I administered Holy Viaticum, she inspired us all, and we thanked God she was there.

A few days later Miss Shannon was on the sick list. I inquired for her in the ward and the soldier patients said she too had come down with the dreaded disease. I found her in a room in the main building under the care of her best friend who had offered to be her nurse.

The word got around that Miss Shannon had made what appeared to be a fatal sacrifice for her patients. How they missed her in that terrible tent! Many a soldier's prayer was said for her and I believe that her bravery bolstered the courage of the sick men who knew her. They acquired a new "will to live," and it is possible her saintly ministry among them bestowed fresh hope and a purpose to carry on, for her sake.

The doctors admired her, and they were wholeheartedly solicitous for her comfort. The commanding officer of the hospital told me that he intended to recommend Miss Shannon for the Distinguished Service Medal.

He was deeply impressed by her genuine heroism. I have always been thankful that he suggested one day that I go aboard the transports and get oranges, for they were hard to find in France. One day I called with a bagful and discovered to my horror that Miss Shannon's nurse was occupying the other bed in the room; she too was a victim of the disease.

When it appeared that the condition of the little nurse was approaching the critical stage she requested that I try to notify her brother who, she said, was in the front line trenches. She hoped to see him before she died.

It seemed impossible to get word to him, for the A.E.F. were then in the throes of a big drive. But her brother came. It all seemed providential, for the moment he arrived Miss Shannon began to regain her strength. Her friend also improved. The lad from the front cheered them with his barrack room stories; he dispensed a spiritual medicine which helped toward their eventual recovery.

The little nurse from North Carolina and her devoted friend became well before I was detached and ordered home. We kept the soldier brother informed of her progress, and the men of the wards heard one day that the beloved red-head was sitting in the sun and yearning to go back to work.

The story was told. I believe I enjoyed recalling that incident more than did my hearers. But the old priest spoke up.

"Did you say, Father, that the nurse came from North Carolina?"

"Yes," I replied, "from Raleigh, and I am quite sure her name is Shannon."

The old priest's eyes lighted up, and he dropped his pipe in the ash-tray.

"Shannon," he exclaimed. "Why, I baptized her; I gave her her first Holy Communion; she's the daughter of my dearest friend. I'll certainly tell him about this when I get back to Raleigh. The little nurse is home with her family now, hale and hearty."

I never again met the old pastor of Raleigh but I have often pictured in my mind his visit to the Shannon family. He had a new reason to be proud of the little red-headed nurse—his faithful parishioner.

CHAPTER 15

Rolling Down to Rio

THE police band of New York's "finest" grouped in the bow of a city tug and played "Till We Meet Again" as the *Idaho* stood down the bay heading for the Narrows and the romantic task of "rolling down to Rio." For all practical purposes the immaculate *Idaho* had become a private yacht. Our thoughts were on our mission: a safe and pleasant voyage for the President of Brazil and his party.

On the quarterdeck our first morning at sea, Madame Pessoa asked the captain:

"Where is the swimming pool?"

The captain evasively inquired, "When would you and the other ladies care to swim?"

"About three o'clock."

"Very well, Madame, the pool will be ready at three."

Captain Vogelgesang pleaded pressing business and descended the ladder near his cabin. He sent for the ship's carpenter. At five bells in the afternoon watch, Madame Pessoa, her daughter and several ladies of the official party frolicked in one of the best sea-going pools I have ever seen. It was a huge wooden box, lined with canvas. A salt-water hose kept it full to the brim. When the ladies retired from their swim we officers took a dip. The men followed gayly after.

We held smokers and Happy Hours en route to Rio,

but the big event of the voyage was "crossing the line" when we ceremoniously converted polliwogs into shell-backs. This was the first of my four round trips over Neptune's mythical frontier, and I was well lathered by the royal barbers, paddled by his pirates and after being tossed into the tank, manhandled by the polar bears—all in the presence of our laughing guests from Brazil.

One afternoon in the South Atlantic, we sighted a lone sailing ship flying the American ensign, wrong side up— a signal of distress—maybe a mutiny. We changed course, and soon drew alongside the lonely schooner. We offered help but the bewhiskered old skipper merely asked us to give our position. He wasn't quite sure where he was; he said he was bound for Lisbon. Otherwise all was well. Apparently the old sea dog wanted only a close-up view of Uncle Sam's newest "Queen of the Seas."

The Brazilian fleet met the *Idaho* far out at sea and escorted us to the magnificent Bay of Guanabara, the harbor of Rio de Janeiro. The people of this beautiful city gave us a royal reception. The American colony entertained the crew at the country club. We officers, what with tennis matches in the morning, golf in the afternoon and official dinners at night, were virtually, as someone put it, "recreated to death." But we liked it. And the people of Rio came to the ship in droves. The day we sailed, a group of prep school boys whom I had taken on a tour of the ship, gave me a crystal the size of a tennis ball. Inside was a statuette of the Blessed Virgin Mary, wrought in Brazilian gold. Their leader made a gracious speech in English.

I shall always remember the reception the ship gave the President of Brazil, government dignitaries, army and navy leaders and the diplomatic corps, whose dean was the Papal Nuncio. The captain assigned me to look after the distinguished group of ecclesiastics. It was fortunate that they spoke French as it gave me a chance to answer their many inquiries about the ship and navy way of living.

After a tour of topside I showed them the crew's reception room, and I startled them when I said that twenty or more received Holy Communion daily and that many others assisted every morning at Holy Mass. It surprised them too that I was the only chaplain on board; the Papal Nuncio approved of the general service I conducted for those of the Protestant faith.

Among the interesting Brazilians I met in Rio was Father Nabuco who is now the Bishop of Petropolis. His brother was a member of the president's party and a fine shipmate. I dined at the Nabuco home and had fun pretending that I was ignorant of their dispensation from Friday abstinence. Like the people of Portugal who have enjoyed the privilege since the days of the Crusades, Brazilians are not required to abstain from meat on Friday. Several courses of meat were served the Friday I was their guest, and I pretended to be shocked. They must have taken me quite seriously, for at the president's reception a few days later, one of the Nabuco girls persuaded the American ambassador, Mr. Edwin Morgan, to explain in his best diplomatic way the nation's dispensation. Some day I hope to explain to Bishop Nabuco, should I ever have the luck to return to beautiful Rio, that I was merely taking his charming family for a "ride."

From the South Atlantic the *Idaho* proceeded to Colon and passed through the Panama Canal, joining the newly organized Pacific Fleet at Monterey, California. At sea, the football squad had a daily work-out on the quarter-deck. When we fell in with the others, they were primed for the kick-off. As we steamed past the battleships to take our assigned berth in the bay, the *Mississippi* greeted us with their band and with hundreds of cheering sailors. They rigged a huge banner on an after barbette with the legend: "Welcome, Sister *Idaho*." Our respective crews became great friends. We officers of the *Idaho* beat the *Mississippi* to the punch that day by promptly inviting their captain and ship's officers to a buffet luncheon. Our chief petty officers also gave a party for the "*Missy*" chiefs. When we got to San Francisco, they held, as always, a gala reception to the Fleet. At luncheon in the wardroom one Easter Sunday, the late Major William B. Sullivan, who commanded the ship's marine detachment, spoke to me.

"Padre, let's go over and see the New York Giants play the Seals."

"Can do," I replied.

The assistant engineering officer, Lieutenant Commander David I. Hedrick, who recently commanded the cruiser *Minneapolis*, saw a chance to pull my leg.

He caustically remarked, "That's a fine place for the padre to be going on Easter Sunday."

Commander Frank R. McCrary, the executive officer, carried the ball from there.

"Don't let Hedrick get your goat, padre," he said. "It reminds me of a Sunday in Manila. I was having lunch with the admiral when his orderly announced that a chaplain had come to see him on important business that couldn't wait.

" 'Send him in,' said the admiral."

McCrary repeated the dialogue between the commander-in-chief of the Asiatic Fleet and the chaplain.

" 'I've come, Sir, to protest against Sunday baseball.' The chaplain's eyes were flashing. 'The team from my ship is scheduled to play in Manila this afternoon.'

"The admiral asked, 'How long have you been in the Navy, chaplain?'

" 'Three months, Sir, I just arrived out here.'

" 'I suggest you talk this over with some of the older and more experienced chaplains.'

" 'I'll do that, Sir, if you'll tell me where I can find them.'

" 'You'll find Father Rainey playing first base and Father Gleeson umpiring. You'd better come along with me.' "

On the morning of Good Friday, 1920, the *Idaho* moored at a pier in the Navy Yard, Bremerton, Washington. I was sitting in my room reading the recently delivered mail, interviewing men who were about to go on emergency leave, greeting Y secretaries who came with offers of hospitality for the crew, and doing dozens of other jobs that tend to keep the wolf—tedium—from a chaplain's door. In the midst of this especially chaotic mélange of activities, a tall, robust, ruddy priest entered the room suddenly like a fresh breeze from the pine woods, and shouted, "Good morning, Bill, I'm Father Camerman." Here was the celebrity I had heard so much about, the ecclesiastical Paul Bunyan of the North Country.

I had been told that he was a pastor in Bremerton before

he went overseas as a chaplain in the Army. He had faced the enemy's guns in the Argonne Forest. He had visited his birthplace in Flanders after the armistice, proud of his commission in the A.E.F. Here was a priest I had long wanted to know.

Father Camerman soon got down to business. "Will you preach for me tonight?"

Feeling that I was not well enough prepared to address a civilian congregation, I parried, "Thank you. But I'm holding services for the crew on board tonight."

But—I changed the hour of the ship's services and delivered a Good Friday sermon to Father Camerman's Bremerton flock. Father Joe later invited me to the rectory, a little frame house a block from the church. So many people came to him with their troubles and good wishes that we were much delayed in getting there. We chatted for a while, and then I asked my colorful host what he did during off hours.

"Well," he smiled, "I have a few hobbies. Come, I'll show you my work-bench." He led me to the cellar and showed me an elaborate array of glistening tools.

"What's it for?" I asked, drawing him out.

"Oh, I build boats and repair things. I built that room over there." He broke out a fistful of keys and opened the door of a large room that filled the corner of the cellar.

It was the most attractive den I had ever seen. On the deck and hanging on the walls were bear skins, whose original owners had inhabited the near-by woods. There were stuffed mountain lions and mounted steel-heads. And along the walls were cases of guns of various calibers and racks for fishing tackle. Sitting in his trophy room, Father Joe told me of a recent foray in the north woods

when he had treed a big bear. The grizzly had climbed
to the top of a tall tree. When the padre again shot him,
the big beast lost his balance and crashed to the ground
less than a foot from where the hunter stood. Father
Camerman admitted it was a "close shave."

I am proud to have had something to do with getting
Father Camerman into the Navy as a lieutenant comman-
der of the chaplain corps. In spite of war service in the
A.E.F. the heart of this great priest has always been in the
Navy.

The *Idaho* was the answer to the prayer of sailors who
"joined the Navy to see the world." We had been the
first battleship to visit Alaska, anchoring in Katchmak
Bay, a stone's throw from a glacier. Our mission was to
meet the Secretary of the Navy and take him back to the
States. While there, I picked up a fine bear skin from an
Eskimo woman on the dock near a "ghost" village. I
later had it cured and mounted in Seattle.

In September, 1920, the *Idaho* paid a visit to the
Hawaiian Islands. I greatly enjoyed my first visit to
Honolulu and Hilo. The volcano of Kilauea was in active
eruption. We made up a large party of officers and men,
arriving at the crater before sunset and staying on to view
the mammoth fireworks in the dark. One of the bluejackets was heard to exclaim, "Gosh, if Hell's like that,
I'm gonna be good."

The Fleet visited Valparaiso, Chile, in the summer of
1921. We again staged an elaborate "Neptunus Rex party"
when we crossed the Equator, and being a shellback, I
found the excitement a great deal more enjoyable than
the first time. Lieutenant Commander Daniel J. Callaghan,

assistant gunnery officer, paid the penalty for being an especially popular shipmate by being subjected to all the most barbarous forms of equatorial torture. The members of the ship's raceboat crew, enacting the rôle of polar bears in Neptune's royal pool gave Dan what the men called "the works." Dan Callaghan, since our shipmate days in the *Idaho*, has been a dear friend. In the spring of 1938, when he was operations officer on the staff of Rear Admiral Joseph K. Taussig, I drove him one evening to the Biltmore Hotel in Los Angeles where he was to meet Mary, his wife.

When he entered the lobby, he discovered himself being paged. A naval officer on duty in the White House phoned that President Roosevelt had chosen Dan for his naval aide. He served with the President for over two years. He is now in command of the heavy cruiser, *San Francisco*, named for the city of his birth.

At Valparaiso, Father Morales, a prominent Chilean priest, boarded the flagship as a delegate of President Allessandro to extend an invitation to the doctors and chaplains of the Fleet to spend four days in Santiago inspecting activities in which they had a professional interest. Chaplain John W. Moore and I made the tour together, visiting schools and social service institutions. The newspapers interviewed us exhaustively, but the Chilean government rewarded us with the Order of Merit. I still proudly wear the ribbon on my service blouse.

The chaplains of the Fleet in those days worked in close harmony on our common spiritual mission. The same condition exists today. In the early twenties Chaplain John Moore, and later his successor in the *Mississippi*, Chaplain Frank Lash, frequently exchanged ships with me on Sunday mornings. I celebrated early Mass in the *Idaho* and then went to the *Mississippi*, where, thanks to the efforts of the Protestant chaplain, I always found a large congregation waiting. The *Idaho* too turned out hundreds to greet their "guest" chaplain. I believe there is today in the navy chaplain corps the highest degree of religious tolerance and coöperation.

In the early twenties, life in the Fleet was far less Spartan than it is today. Instead of nightly blackouts at sea, our evenings under a tropic moon were delightful. If we were not laughing at the Mack Sennett comedies of the silent screen, and finding our movie favorites charming though mute, we played on our mandolins and guitars and sang the salty ballads of the sailor.

It surprises my younger friends when I tell of a race that five battleships ran from Santa Barbara to San Pedro in the spring of 1920. It started with a discussion among officers ashore regarding the relative merits of the engineering plants in the various ships. The morning we left Santa Barbara, they lined up the ships like thoroughbreds on a track, and when the flagship, *New Mexico*, hoisted the signal, they took off—to let the best battle wagon win. A few minutes after the *Idaho* hit her stride we assembled in the stern the blaring band and hundreds of rollicking, raucous sailors to make their weight lower the "wheels" in the water and give the Queen of the Seas added speed. We won, with our sister ship, the *Mississippi*, a close second. The crew promptly hoisted swabs on the trucks and cheered derisively at the other ships as they limped to their anchorages.

Racing on the water reminds me of the fleet regatta, held that summer in the harbor of Los Angeles. Again it was a matter of the *Idaho* or the *Missy* winning the big race of the day. As he stood on the quarterdeck, with his senior officers, Captain Vogelgesang expressed his full confidence in his crew. The sailors had placed thousands of dollars on the race; it was do or die. After the race, when our beaten crew came aboard, the captain sent for them and congratulated each man on his faithful efforts. He also said that he believed the *Mississippi's* boat was non-regulation, and he asked the crew if they would be willing to pull the race again. Then he had the officer of the deck call away his gig and went to the *Mississippi* where he argued the point with Captain Moffett, the *Missy's* commanding officer. The latter said that he was not only sure that the *Missy's* boat was regulation in every respect but that they would gladly race again, this time using the *Idaho's* boat. They beat us fairly the second time but our captain had convinced the crew that he believed in them.

During my cruise in the *Idaho*, I served on the staff of Major Harold F. Wirgman, U.S.M.C. as chaplain of the Fleet marine regiment. It gave me my only chance to serve directly under a marine officer and that for only a short time when the marines of the Pacific Fleet encamped for a few weeks on Catalina Island. Whenever the marines were not ridding the island of wild goats with their rifles, they practiced landing from boats through the surf and other drills for which the "leather-neck" is famous.

When the time came for me to round up talent for a campfire smoker, I discovered that the enlisted man of the marine corps is temperamentally different from his brother-in-arms, the bluejacket. It would have been an easy task to corral a troupe of sailors to perform, but it took considerable persuasion to entice the dignified marine to assume the rôle of a vaudeville performer. I finally made up a program, and we put on a Happy Hour for the men sitting around the camp fire, the night before we broke camp and embarked for the Fleet.

As a member of "Wirgie's" staff, I roomed in a little cottage, on Catalina Island, with Dr. Joseph J. Kaveney who snored so prodigiously that I usually, after he had struck the right note and rhythm, picked up my mattress and flemished down on the kitchen floor. The adjutant, Captain Lewie G. Merritt and I, started the day together with a brisk run of a mile across the peninsula and took a dip in the surf, and then ran back again. One day following a regimental drill, Captain Merritt sent for a marine who, he noticed, limped as he passed in review. When Lewie asked the man what the trouble was, he replied, "I hurt my knee, Cap." Merritt's temper hit the sky.

"What do you mean by calling me 'Cap'?" The lad pointed to his knee and explained, "It's here, Sir, my kneecap." Lieutenant Colonel Lewie Merritt is now an aviator in command of the Twenty-First Marine Defense Squadron at Ewa, Hawaii. A few weeks ago he flew me in his bomber over the top of the volcano Mauna Loa. While losing altitude rather rapidly, Lewie asked whether it was affecting my ears. I replied, "My ears are all right, but I hurt my knee—Cap." I can still hear him laugh through the ear-phones.

In one's naval career there is bound to be a ship for which a navy man has especial affection. I loved the

Idaho. I helped put her in commission and I observed her officers and men put a soul into her. The captain made it clear how important it was that we make the *Idaho* shine from truck to keel. We quickly developed high pride in our ship and we were gratified years later that she continued to have an excellent reputation in the battle line.

The morning the ship was commissioned—the first of her life in the Navy, I felt rather hurt that I, the ship's chaplain, had not been included in the ceremony. It was the first time I had witnessed the commissioning of a navy ship and I felt that religion somehow should be included. I went quietly to my room and got my ritual, stole, and a small bottle of holy water, and climbed to the maintop alone. Standing there, I blessed the ship and solemnly prayed the Blessed Virgin Mary to protect the *Idaho's* officers and men from harm. I told no one about this for many years, but it did not seem strange to me that the *Idaho* escaped the tragedies that befell her sister ships, the *Mississippi* and *New Mexico*. Fourteen years later I joined the *Mississippi* which had recently been modernized and recommissioned; and while cruising off the coast of Maine, a young officer was killed at his gun. That same afternoon, I told my friend Barry Wilson, the gunnery officer, about the day in Camden when I blessed our sister ship. He said, "Padre mio, get your book and stole and come with me. It can't do any harm."

CHAPTER 16

Shore Duty

It was inevitable that I should one day be ordered to duty at a shore station. I had become accustomed to life in a ship—its well-ordered routine, bracing discipline, the thrill of getting under way for a week or more at sea and the anticipation of stepping ashore at the end of a voyage in places invitingly new. It was unnatural to be suddenly separated from it. I liked being near the men, to have the chance to know them and to help them in their problems. It was interesting to organize committees which the crew elected to assume responsibilities in connection with ship's dances, Happy Hours and picnics.

A chaplain's desk in his room at sea is like a table in front of a boulevard café. All during the day officers and men pass "on their lawful occasions" and wave a greeting or stop for a smoke and a chat. The chaplain has his hand on the ship's pulse; he "savvies" the men's thoughts and he knows how to keep them contented. What he picks up during a busy day on the "boulevard" he can judiciously, in his capacity as an aide for morale to the executive officer, lend a helpful hand in many ways. Men are usually frank with the chaplain if the latter is a genuine, prudent friend. A word dropped casually to a division officer can often place a man in a position to go ahead in the direction of a rating in which he may do his best work. A chaplain, when a good buffer between the crew and the officers, is of inestimable value to the ship.

I have made many lasting friendships among the Navy's enlisted men and I have found saints among them whose spirituality, under the circumstances, was amazing.

When the Fleet was at Panama in 1939, Chaplain Frank H. Lash, an Episcopal minister serving as battle force chaplain, came aboard my ship, the cruiser *Indianapolis*, and told me of one of his shipmates in the *California*. He said he wanted me to speak with one of his sailors who desired to become a Trappist monk. Chaplain Lash suggested that I talk to the lad before letters were written in recommendation. I went aboard the *California* with Frank and met the man in the chaplain's room. The sailor said he had aspired for a long time to the holy life of a cloistered monk. He had become a vegetarian and abstained from other items of a sailor's usual diet to find out whether or not he was equal to it. He had trained himself to wake up in his hammock in the middle of the night to recite his rosary. But he did not have the appearance of an ascetic; in fact, he had all the ear marks of a typical machinist's mate—rugged, rough and ready. That young man is now in a Trappist monastery in Kentucky.

I was driving along Wilshire Boulevard in Los Angeles three years ago; it was seventeen years after I had left the *Idaho*. A man driving a truck behind me was trying to attract my attention so I turned down the next side street and stopped the car. The truck drew up alongside and the driver jumped down with outstretched hand. It was Jack Thornton, my talented yeoman of the *Idaho* days. I was in uniform, having driven Chaplain Father Edward E.

Duff to the city on an official mission. It thrilled me to meet him again. We rapidly reminisced on our shipmate adventures and inquired about old friends. Nor was I surprised when he pathetically told me that he often spent his Sunday afternoons driving his wife and children to the Long Beach landing where he waited, hoping to run across an old shipmate; his heart was still in the Navy. I have met old sailor friends everywhere, even on the streets of New York. Not long ago, I ran across a navy man in Los Angeles whom I first knew as a chief pharmacists mate in one of the hospitals at Brest. He is Frank Law, now president of the John B. Wyeth Company of Philadelphia. Frank reached the top.

Since shore duty does not lend itself so readily to the forming of friendships as does life aboard a navy ship, I was not enthusiastic about my orders to the Naval Training Station at Great Lakes, Illinois. But I found work plentiful among the eight thousand officers and men who then were stationed in that picturesque place on the shores of Lake Michigan. I lived in Waukegan and enjoyed frequent visits with the Burkes and the Mackins. Mr. John Machin, in those days, was a devotee of cock fighting. He thought I also was an enthusiast for I humored him by attending the weekly "mains" he held in his barn. Men of sporting habits came even from New Orleans to match their fighting cocks against Mr. Mackin's game gladiators. The Mackins' only son, Father Tom, now a pastor in South Carolina, thought his father must be a "throw-back" to some wild Irish ancestor. I never discovered what Father Tom thought of me and my apparent interest in that peculiar sport. Mrs. Mackin once told me (I have wondered how I managed to keep a straight face), that her wealthy husband came to the drawing room one afternoon when she was entertaining ladies at tea. He was dressed in clothes which he had worn on the day of their marriage. He bowed gallantly to the ladies and then revealed why he had kept his hands behind his back by releasing two game cocks that put on a ferocious bout right there on the Turkish rug. Mr. Mackin had color. He liked to talk about the days when he boxed with Champion John L. Sullivan. Before I left, he presented me with a thoroughbred Airedale. I dubbed him "Spike" after my Seton Hall roommate, Father Walter "Spike" Hennesy.

I stayed there fourteen months and then asked the Navy Department to send me to sea. Someone must have told my friend Captain Frank Taylor Evans. He wrote asking whether I would like to assist him in putting the Newport training station in commission. It was like a pat on the back. Soon I was driving my Dodge roadster over the rough, unfinished roads of Indiana and I used up three tires. My sister, Anita, met me at Buffalo and we drove to Bethlehem, detouring to Elmira, where I had spent my boyhood. I told Anita of my preference for sea duty, deploring the idea of living alone in an apartment. I had grown fond of the club atmosphere of the *Idaho* wardroom. To my surprise, my sister volunteered to be my hostess. She had recently completed her studies at Mount Saint Mary's College in New Jersey. It was there I first heard the angelic voice of Jessica Dragonette. She and Anita were classmates. It was settled. I would take a house and Anita would run it in harmony with all she had absorbed in her domestic science course at school.

In the fall of 1921, Anita, Spike and I set up housekeeping in an attractive cottage not far from the public beach at Newport, Rhode Island. It was a novel experience fraught with extraordinary possibilities. I had never known that rats die within house walls. Nor did I know that it is difficult to heat a Newport cottage during a typical Down East winter.

We entertained in a simple way. Anita often invited school friends to visit her. Almost daily I introduced unexpected guests at the dinner table; but our cook was patient and fairly efficient. One of our frequent visitors was Dr. Roger A. Nolan, now a commander in the medical corps. He and Anita were married the following October.

My colleague at the training station was Chaplain Emil Groth, a Lutheran minister of wide erudition. We had already become fast friends in Chaplain Isaacs' "make ye learn" school in the Brooklyn Navy Yard. It pleased me to be again with my good friend. He had a sound common-sense philosophy and a delightful sense of fun. We saw eye to eye on things pertaining to our daily tasks. We were virtually inseparable. The people of Newport called him "Father," and this prompted me to tell him this story which he enjoyed. It ran something like this: A group of St. Mary's altar boys were playing one morning on a Jersey City sidewalk. Maybe it was marbles, if the cops were near. A minister wearing a Roman collar came up the street and one of the boys arose to greet him. "Good morning, Father." The minister stopped and chatted a moment with the boy and proceeded on his way. When the lad rejoined the group, one of his playmates exclaimed, "What d'ya mean callin' him 'Father'? He ain't no Father —he's got five kids."

Chaplain Groth was ready with a sequel. We both had

been fortunate that cold winter in winning the affection of the sailor who distributed soft coal for our furnaces. He contrived to obtain large handy chunks by personally supervising the loading of his truck. One day he announced to Chaplain Groth that he expected he would soon be transferred to sea. "Chaplain, your coal ain't gonna be so good any more. The guy what's gonna relieve me is a blamed Protestant."

We revived an old custom at Newport of holding morning prayers at eight o'clock on the "grinder"—the drill grounds where the recruits were trained in infantry drill. Emil and I took turns. When the chaplain arrived, the men were assembled in front of the reviewing stand and they stood reverently while he conducted a brief service. After prayers, they marched in review; the chaplain at salute acknowledging the "eyes right" as they smartly marched by. I discovered, to my dismay, in 1935, that this splendid custom had gone by the board.

In addition to personal interviews in my office and lectures to the recruit companies, I had the attractive assignment of reviving the *Newport Recruit*—the station weekly. It was a little thing of four pages but it was newsy and it also carried a picture of the week's honor man and a short story of his triumph. The men were encouraged to write articles and to collect human interest stories about their shipmates. I was busy on the first number of the *Recruit* when chief boatswain's mate, "Frenchy" Le Roy, a weather-beaten survivor of the "old" Navy, came to my office. "Frenchy," in his early days, had been the coxswain of Admiral "Fighting Bob" Evans' barge. He later shifted his loyal allegiance to the admiral's son, with whom he had recently served in France. "Frenchy," with all his faults, was a good drill master, requiring of his charges that they train for a hard life in what was unmistakably the "hard way." But he knew all the answers and he usually gave them gruffly in the salty manner acquired in the rugged school of the sea.

I was glad to see "Frenchy." I rather thought he might have some "angles" for the ship's paper. In my desire to learn naval lore, I welcomed his visits although I used to feel a bit humble in his presence.

"Frenchy" looked over my shoulder. "What's ya got there, Father?"

"Galley proofs for the first *Recruit*."

"Are ya gonna run ads?"

Feeling I had made an irreparable blunder, I tried to assure him that ads would be unnecessary; the welfare fund would be equal to the strain.

"But Father Gleeson used to have ads when he ran the *Recruit*. I used to work for him when I was a boot in training," he said. He told the following yarn about his first job as a newspaper man. One day Father Gleeson sent for "Frenchy" and directed him to scour the country-side for ads and not to return until he had obtained a bucketful. "Frenchy" labored for three days and three nights, covering Newport, Fall River and Providence. He finally returned to the station, looking, he admitted, like the wreck of the *Hesperus*, but his pockets were bulging with ads and they were all paid for. When Father Gleeson discovered that his *Recruit* had won the patronage of every saloon keeper on "Frenchy's" itinerary, which embraced a special detour to a Providence brewery, he nearly fainted. He ordered "Frenchy" to shove off immediately and return the money. But it took the bewildered sailor three days to complete the rounds, having accepted "one on the house" at each stop. This may have accounted for my having to manage somehow to publish the *Recruit* without benefit of commercial propaganda.

I felt too much like a smug civilian in Newport. One day I discovered a chance to join the destroyer squadron in Turkish waters. I asked the Bureau to send me. Orders came and I boarded the U.S.S. *Trinity*, an oil tanker, at Hampton Roads—bound for Constantinople.

CHAPTER 17

Turkish Waters

ON A spring morning in 1925 my friend, Father Joseph T. Casey, who was then serving at the Norfolk training station, drove me to the landing at the operating base to report for duty on board the U.S.S. *Trinity* for passage to Constantinople, Turkey. I had never before gone to sea in a tanker, but rather liked the idea of the long, uninterrupted haul to Gibraltar. It meant hours for reading all the books I had taken along. The ship was crowded with officers and men, passengers like myself, with orders to the Turkish station. Congress in those days appropriated little money for transportation of naval personnel. We were packed in the *Trinity* like money in a billfold. My cot was so placed in the passageway that every time the messenger came in the night watches to the executive officer's room, he stumbled over me. So, frequently I'd say, "Oh, that's all right," before the sailor had a chance to apologize.

It felt good, finally, to be anchored in the Bosphorus and to see the lights glimmering on the great mosques, beyond the Golden Horn. It was the season of Ramazan, and we found it interesting to watch the "whirling" dervishes and the less refined "howling" dervishes who did marvelous stunts under a spell, a sort of hypnosis. After repeating the word, "Bismalah," countless times in dreary monotone, they became drowsy and strangely innured to physical pain. They were able then to bite into burning charcoal and stick daggers into their flesh without flinching.

My original orders to the tender *Denebola* were changed; Rear Admiral Mark Bristol directed me to report on board the "beef boat," *Bridge*. The *Denebola's* chaplain, a Christian Scientist, still had a large fund to expend for Armenian refugees. The Mother Church in Boston apparently arranged to have his orders revoked in order to give him an opportunity to finish his philanthropic assignment.

One afternoon the skipper of the *Bridge*, Commander Kittinger, invited me to accompany him to a conference of commanding officers which Captain Arthur J. Hepburn frequently conducted in his office, near the American embassy. When the captain asked me what I thought of my duties in the destroyer force, I requested a roving commission in the destroyers in order to become better acquainted with the men. Much to my delight, he approved. Immediately Lieutenant Commander John B. Rhodes invited me to join him in the *Litchfield* on a cruise in the Black Sea. Lieutenant Commander James G. Ware, the admiral's flag secretary, said he would issue the orders. It soon became a habit with Ware.

The following morning I was standing on the bridge of the *Litchfield* as she steamed through the Bosphorus to the Black Sea on a course that took us to Varna, Bulgaria. I found the Bulgarians interesting. They seemed to dress equally well or poorly, depending on one's point of view. They were poor but healthy. The leading dentist of Varna, a graduate of the University of Pennsylvania, who had an inordinate fondness for doughnuts, frequently came aboard. He had spent several months as a war prisoner in Roumania, a subject that was always on his mind. One night in the wardroom he confessed he had no love for his neighbors across the frontier.

One afternoon Rhodes and I went ashore for a walk. We were strolling through one of the attractive parks of the town when a Russian boy, who could not have been more than fifteen, came up to us and handed the captain a letter. It had been written by a bartender in the Casino. It went something like this: "Dear Mr. Captain: This guy is the son of a Cossack general. How's to give him a job on your boat?" It had an unmistakable American touch.

Rhodes took a fancy to the lad and wrote a few words on the letter. Then he told him to take the letter to the ship. Our Russian waif, who was as bright as a modern "Quiz Kid," rapidly became the best seaman in the fo'c'sle division. Having studied before the revolution in the Don Cadet School, he quickly learned to read and speak English. One night he told me what had happened to his family. His father, before he was killed in action, had been a prominent general in command of a Cossack cavalry regiment. His mother and sister had died during the exodus from their home in Kiev. The boy had been taken as a refugee to a British camp in Egypt. He and several other Russian boys had recently been shipped to Bulgaria. The sailors called the youngster, "Pete," and when orders were given to discharge all Russian waifs, they held a tarpaulin muster and collected enough money to buy Pete a passage to New York where he waited several months until the *Litchfield* returned to the United States. The *Litchfield* sailors practically adopted the boy;

they bought his clothes and paid the doctor's bills. Not being an American citizen, Pete was unable to enlist in the Navy. He finally joined the coast guard, and when I last heard from him he was a radio man first class, serving in a destroyer and married to "a little Irish girl in Flatbush." I was in the *Mississippi* at the time and got a visual message from Pete one day when the ship was leaving Hampton Roads.

Several destroyers on the Turkish station adopted Russian refugees and made them members of the ship's company until the admiral put a stop to the custom. The *McCormick* once had a Russian prince who worked in the ship's laundry.

I seldom stayed long in the *Bridge*. Living, as it were, out of a suitcase, I went on several voyages to Black Sea ports and to interesting little places like Dideagatch and Kavalla in Macedonia. We frequently anchored off Mudros, the bleak little town where the brave Anzacs had assembled before they began their fight in the Dardanelles campaign.

On New Year's Eve at Mudros, word came to the division commander that a boat which had set out with our chief pharmacist's mate who was to attend a sick man in one of the other ships, had failed to return. There was a blizzard raging, and the visibility was so poor that one could not make out an object twenty feet away. Our three destroyers steamed all that night in the blinding snow, hoping to find the missing men. The next morning the weather suddenly cleared, and the quartermaster sighted a boat standing toward the ship. Having luckily reached shore the crew had spent the night in a shack where they shared a loaf of bread with a deserter from the Greek army. When the pharmacist's mate came aboard, still shivering and soaked to the skin, he replied to the captain's greeting: "Sir, I'm so glad to be back, I'm glad I went."

In early January dispatch orders sent the destroyers, *McCormick* and *Simpson* on a wild dash to the Black Sea in search of an American merchantman reported lost in a storm. That was the roughest sea trip I have ever made. As we headed into mountainous seas, an especially big one crashed over us and broke the glass ports of the navigation bridge, cutting the men on watch. For several days we searched the waters of the Black Sea and found no trace of the missing vessel. It was then decided to visit every town on the southern coast from Batoum in Georgia to the Turkish town of Samsoon.

No reply came to our message to Moscow asking permission to enter the port of Batoum. The captain felt that in the circumstances, he was justified in going there to seek information about the wreck. Several mean little commissars came aboard soon after we dropped anchor and told us, with the aid of an aristocratic interpreter, to leave the bay or be fired upon. They were ugly and would tell us nothing.

From Batoum the ship stopped wherever a village appeared on the chart. My knowledge of French earned me the privilege of going ashore with the captain to ask the French-speaking army officers what they knew regarding the lost merchantman. Usually the good-natured Turks met us in the offshore surf and carried us piggy-back to the beach. There were no docks. Occasionally we stayed long enough to enjoy a cup of strong coffee with the Turkish officers. We kept this up until we reached Samsoon; but no trace was ever found of the lost ship. It pleased me to know what pains the Navy will take in the interests of our brothers of the merchant marine.

The popularity of the destroyer *McCormick* in the Near East was due in a great measure to the ability of the ship's orchestra to play for dancing ashore. They played well with a certain authentic swing that endeared them to lovers of American jazz. One evening on a cruise to Athens, our sailors played at a dinner dance in the Athens personnel house of the Near East Relief Society. Among those present were professors from Robert College of Constantinople, and Dr. John Finley, the distinguished educator from New York. The next day the professors took passage in the *McCormick* to Beirut, Syria, where they were to take part in the Commencement exercises of the American College. At the general service, which preceded Mass on Sunday morning at sea, the orchestra played for the congregational singing. It amused the professors to hear the sailors render "Onward Christian Soldiers" as only a popular jazz orchestra could play it. After church they broke out their fountain pens and wrote home about it.

I enjoyed many interesting talks with Dr. John Finley. His personal charm equaled his extraordinary erudition. One day at sea we stood on the *McCormick's* bridge as we neared the town of Chanak in the Dardanelles. The country reminded him of Homer and this in turn led to the general topic of poetry. He recalled a day when he stood on a hill overlooking Jerusalem. Where he stood, there were three crosses marking the graves of British soldiers who had been killed in Allenby's command. It inspired Dr. Finley to write a little poem he called "On the Quest." I told him I hoped to read it some day. He promptly left the bridge and went to his room and inscribed the poem for me. He also drew a little sketch of the scene in the upper corner of the page. After he gave it to me he said he had sent copies to the mothers of the men whose names appeared on the crosses. The poem has been lost, but I trust it will reach me some day when Dr. Finley's collected poems are published.

One day during Lent I was having lunch at the club in Constantinople when Lieutenant Commander Richard S. Field asked me when I intended giving his Catholic men a chance to make their Easter duty. Not knowing his ship was in port I asked when it would be convenient for him to arrange for confessions and Mass. I have found this sort of interest in the spiritual welfare of the men to be typical of the American line officer. Field's ship was then in an Italian floating drydock at Stenia on the Bosphorus. The following day I boarded a steamer, which was loaded to the gunwales with Turks and Armenians, and went to the ancient town where Jason and his shipmates are said to have made a mythological liberty.

The jovial Dick Field, who was the idol of his crew, met me at the gangway, led me down the ladder to his cabin, and right back again to the welldeck where his men stood to hear what their skipper had to say. Field had given orders for this assembly when he saw me approaching the dock. He told the crew that I had come to offer Mass on board and to administer Holy Communion; then he added that I was also anxious to serve the Protestant men and they might see me in his cabin that evening. In his introduction he gave me a flattering "build-up," and then asked me to say a few words. What I told the crew that day I have forgotten, but it was gratifying to see so many men at Mass on the navigation bridge the next morning. At the Offertory of the Mass, a muezzin, in gown and turban, appeared on top of a near-by minaret and intoned his weird call to prayer. It was competition of an unusual sort but it only increased our regard for Captain Field's thoughtfulness.

At another place Mass was offered under quite different observation. At dawn on a Sunday morning in July, the *McCormick* arrived at Odessa. The men rigged for church on the fo'c'sle; the altar was placed at the forward end, and chairs and benches were arranged on either side of the four-inch gun. By seven o'clock, when Mass began, the Reds from the town had heard of our arrival and came out in small boats to look at us. They came so close that I could feel them staring. Had they known, they would have been impressed at seeing Colonel Haskell, U. S. Army, his son a West Point cadet, Foster Stearns a secretary of the embassy, Lieutenant Anton Mare, Ensign William Fitzgerald and several sailors receiving Holy Communion. The Bolsheviks down in their row boats might have learned something about the American procedure of living.

A few months after I arrived at Constantinople, Admiral Mark Bristol, the high commissioner, knowing how much I liked going to sea with destroyer men, ordered me to the *McCormick* for duty as chaplain of the Thirty-ninth Division. Being now a permanent member of the ship's company and senior to Lieutenant Raymond Tarbuck, they gave me, in spite of my protests, his room, the little one outboard of the wardroom ladder, the cabin usually assigned to the chief engineer. It made it convenient for the men to drop in for a chat and a smoke. I was proud to be the only chaplain ever to have a permanent billet in a destroyer. Roving among the ships of the famous Thirty-ninth gave me the most attractive opportunities I have ever enjoyed for serving the men of the Navy.

The *McCormick* was a splendid little four-stacker, and her crew the finest I have ever been shipmates with. They kept the ship immaculate and their spirit was as high as her marks in gunnery. Each sailor had an important job; the business of keeping up the ship always took precedence, in the minds of the crew, over "hitting the beach." I recall our arriving at Naples after a week of heavy weather. The men refused the privilege of going ashore until they had the "*Micky*" sparkling like a star. She had a winning base-ball team in spite of the fact that I played first base. But Lieutenant Oliver O. "Scrappy" Kessing, the executive officer, played in right field, and this helped a great deal. Under the guiding hand of the leading bosun's mates, Joe Bush and "Whitey" Larson, the "*Micky*" rated at all times the title of "smart ship."

One day when the ship was at Beirut, Syria, General Weygand, the French high commissioner, came aboard for a reception we tendered him and his fellow officers. All afternoon, the famous general of France pretended he spoke no English, but at the gangway, when he was about to go over the side, he turned to the division commander and said, without the trace of an accent: "Captain, I congratulate you. You have a smart ship." He knew this to be the highest compliment.

On Christmas Eve, in the Bay of Alexandria, Egypt, officers and men came in their motor dories to attend midnight Mass in the wardroom of the *McCormick*. It was an inspiring way to celebrate the birthday of Christ, their King.

CHAPTER 18

The Captain's Medal

It was in May, 1923, at Constantinople, when nearly every maritime nation of the world flew its flag in that region at the stern of a warship. The Bosphorus was completely in the hands of the Allies; even Spain had a smart cruiser there. Dreadnaughts were anchored within sight of the sultan's palace—a gesture in sea power calculated to be fearful in the eyes of the Turk but reassuring to the other nationals ashore—a guarantee of protection, should one of the daily crises become a catastrophe.

I had recently returned from the Black Sea where our destroyer had sailed to Odessa in the north and to Samsoon on the southern shore. The sinister type of our ship belied its mission, for our task was to build up rather than to destroy the social fabric of unhappy humanity. My roving commission took me on frequent trips into the Black Sea and the eastern Mediterranean.

On the eve of the departure of one of the destroyer divisions to home waters, the *Bainbridge*, under the command of the late Lieutenant Commander W. Atlee Edwards, came alongside the "beef-boat," *Bridge*, for stores, in much the same smart way as she had approached a French transport a few months before, when her captain won the congressional medal of honor.

131

The circumstances were not the same. Yet as I stood on the deck of my own ship I could visualize the other scene. The citation runs:

Lieutenant Commander Edwards placed his vessel alongside the bow of the French military transport *Vihn-Long* (destroyed by fire in the Sea of Marmora) and in spite of several violent explosions . . . maintained his ship in that position until all who were alive were taken on board. Of a total of 495 on board, 482 (men, women and children) were rescued by his coolness, judgment and professional skill, which were combined with a degree of heroism that must reflect new glory on the United States Navy.

This glorious feat of Edwards was still the popular topic of conversation in all the wardrooms of the ships then cruising in Turkish waters.

The extravagant sunset that evening made a beautiful background for the mosque of Saint Sophia and the forest of minarets that flank the far side of the Golden Horn. It was nearly the hour for dinner and I was about to lay below to my stateroom when I discovered an old shipmate on the navigating bridge of Edwards' ship. We exchanged greetings and I accepted his invitation to dinner.

I had never met Atlee Edwards, although his name was known to me long before the episode in the Sea of Marmora. We met in the diminutive wardroom of the *Bainbridge*. He was a man of medium height, with the clear eyes and general poise of the officer of quick and accurate judgment. He had the air of a citizen of the world, but he was free of the cynicism so often noticeable then among our officers who had seen at close range "man's inhumanity to man" in the Levant. One saw life in the raw when the new republic of Turkey was aborning. In spite of the vogue of damning them because of the few who converted the lot of the refugee into an easy avocation, Atlee Edwards still professed sympathy for the Armenians.

As Edwards joined in the jolly repartee of the mess, he unconsciously twirled, with his index finger, a gold medal which hung suspended from his watch chain. His shipmates have since told me that this sort of nervousness was characteristic of him. The medal struck my fancy for it appeared to have an image of a saint in low relief on one side of it. I asked if I might examine it.

"Gladly, padre," he said. "This is my most precious souvenir." The medal was about the size of a half dollar. On the side opposite the one bearing the saint's image was a sketch of a French destroyer in a heavy sea.

"A lovely medal, captain," I said, almost caressing the thing. "Tell me the history of it."

Atlee Edwards told us that when, at the burning of the *Vihn-Long,* all but two of the transport's personnel and passengers had been taken on board the American craft, only the captain and the chaplain of the troops, an old priest of the Dominican order, were left. Edwards stood on the welldeck of his ship and greeted the priest and the French captain as they climbed aboard. His knowledge of French made this function agreeable, especially to those whose lives he had saved. The old priest was amazed at Edwards' accent. It was peculiarly Parisian. Later, in the cabin, after Edwards had personally arranged for the comfort of the survivors, the bearded chaplain asked the American commander how he had acquired his knowledge of French. Then Edwards explained that he had studied as a boy at the Dominican College in Paris. His father was in the diplomatic service. The priest was in ecstasy. *"Tiens!*

Tiens! You, my dear captain, one of our boys. *Mon Dieu!* What won't they say in Paris when they hear of this!" Then with great feeling the old priest detached the medal from his watch chain. "Please accept this, my son, as a souvenir of your heroic service to my people. It is a medal we wore during the great war when I served with the destroyer squadrons in the Mediterranean."

Atlee Edwards was proud of his medal. I am sure that he wore it to his dying day.

I thought of that dinner party in the Bosphorus while at breakfast in the Fleet five years later. We read in the radio press news that Atlee Edwards had died. At the time of his death he was serving as executive officer of the President's yacht, the *Mayflower*. The other officers at the mess table delivered over that page of radio news the finest composite eulogy I have ever heard given to a fellow-man.

CHAPTER 19

Full Honors

IN THE summer of 1923, Lieutenant Commander William D. "Red" Taylor and I were having dinner on the terrace of the Grand Hotel, on the island of Prinkipo, one of a group known as the Princes' Islands. The destroyers of the Thirty-ninth division, part of the American forces in Turkish waters, had completed the long-range gunnery practice in the Sea of Marmora, and had anchored for a week end off Prinkipo. Ordinarily our ships based in the Bosphorus, a stone's throw from the Sultan's palace. Taylor was the executive officer of the U.S.S. *Litchfield*. My ship, at the time, was the U.S.S. *McCormick*, the flagship of the division.

I rather expected Taylor had something important to say when I received his radio message that morning at sea, inviting me to dine with him at the hotel. He had arranged for a small table to assure our being alone.

"Here's something you'll like, padre," said Taylor. "Get orders to join us. Send a dispatch tonight. We sail for Smyrna tomorrow, and it's the real 'McCoy.' . . . You won't regret it." Red's smile revealed that he offered something worth my while.

I recall that a small Viennese orchestra played many waltzes at dinner that evening, and now, when I hear the melodies of Strauss, I can see Taylor sitting opposite me, on the sea side of the terrace, excitedly telling me of the mission of the *Litchfield*.

Long before the outbreak of the first World War (so went his story), a young Greek from the town of Chesme, on the Smyrna peninsula, arrived as an emigrant in Boston. His name was Dilboy, a name probably anglicised from the Greek. He attended school and soon became a typical American boy. I never heard whether his parents accompanied him; he may have lived with relatives, for we found his mother and father living on a farm on the island of Chios.

When the United States entered the World War, Dilboy was among the first to enlist, and he went overseas with the Yankee division. His great chance came in the battle of the Argonne Forest. There Dilboy became a hero, perhaps the greatest hero in the last phase of the war. His citation told of his leading an attack against German pill-boxes, of pressing on, despite a fractured leg and many other wounds, of silencing with grenades, single-handed, a particularly stubborn pill-box which had taken toll of hundreds of his fellows, of Dilboy's death—at the very edge of the enemy's stronghold. The government awarded Dilboy, posthumously, the Congressional Medal of Honor. His old "buddies" in his home town named the American Legion post for him.

Whether or not Dilboy's remains would be left undisturbed in France was a matter for his parents to decide. His old warrior friends hoped they might bury him in the National Cemetery at Arlington, Va. But a decision was made that resulted in the arrival of a flag-draped casket in the town of Chesme, Turkey, where Dilboy's parents and relatives awaited it with justifiable pride. Alas, for the people of Chesme, the war was not over; the Turks, under Mustapha Kemal Pasha were slowly driving the Greek army literally into the sea. The day Dilboy's casket was placed in the local church was the very day the Turks drove the fleeing Greeks before them. No doubt Holy Mass had been celebrated that morning, but by nightfall everything had changed. Dilboy's parents fled with the rest of the town's people; they crossed the bay to Chios. The casket, draped with the Stars and Stripes, was necessarily abandoned where it lay. According to reports which eventually reached the members of the Dilboy Post of the American Legion, the Turks in their momentary madness, desecrated the casket and flag.

The story runs that the Dilboy Post wrote to Senator David I. Walsh who in turn notified the State Department; and they in turn directed Admiral Mark Bristol, the American high commissioner at Constantinople, to investigate and take proper action.

Here is where the *Litchfield* entered the scene. Taylor, half-whispering, continued: "We sail tomorrow afternoon for Smyrna to pick up the American consul and then to Chesme where the Turks are to give us Dilboy's remains, and they will render highest military honors to Dilboy and the flag. You'd better get off that dispatch and come along."

Of course I returned early to the *McCormick* and radioed a request for orders. The reply came in one word: "Affirmative." I climbed aboard the *Litchfield* the following morning.

That evening the little warship steamed toward the glow of a golden sky, where the Dardanelles ushered her into the vast waters of the eastern Mediterranean. The grim craft seemed to sense the unique importance of her mission.

When we arrived off the quay of Smyrna a boat was lowered and sent to the landing where the American consul and his interpreter, a major of the Turkish army, promptly embarked. The ship then got under way for Chesme which lay on the western shore of the peninsula.

We arrived at Chesme after dark with our man o'war lights aglow. We could see, across the bay, the faint lights in the houses of the town of Castro, on the island of Chios, where the Greeks had sought refuge; and there was some evidence of life in Chesme.

Early the next morning a landing force of thirty sailors were mustered on the welldeck; they carried rifles and bayonets. The captain and his party prepared to leave in the gig; the sailors stood by to follow.

The ceremony near the dock in Chesme was solemn and satisfactory. The Turkish soldiers fired volleys and showed as best they could the sincerity of their apology for the insult that had been perpetrated. In all solemnity, our sailors carried Dilboy's casket and laid it on the thwarts of the whaleboat for the short passage to the ship. They then placed it on the welldeck of the *Litchfield*, and a guard of honor stood beside it. Without further ado our ship got under way and steamed across the bay to the island of Chios. It was hoped that the people of Castro were in the dark as to the purpose of our visit. It was of no importance to the town that our only reason for coming was to persuade the parents of Dilboy to permit us to convey their son's remains to Constantinople for further transfer to the United States, and to Arlington Cemetery.

As we neared the breakwater of Castro, we discovered through our binoculars that every roof-top was black with people. The American consul was annoyed: "Who let the cat out of the bag?" But, as we entered the inner harbor, our vast audience arose and cheered and waved flags and handkerchiefs. This too was disconcerting, and we wondered what it was all about. A few minutes after we had dropped anchor, a local official came off in a launch and explained to the captain this extraordinary interest on the part of the populace. The refugees, having seen our man o'war lights the night before, feared the *Litchfield* might be an Italian warship, sent by Mussolini to bombard them; Il Duce had just horrified the world by shelling Corfu, a wild gesture that almost brought on war with Greece. But when they saw the Stars and Stripes flying at our main, they said, "Thank God, an American ship, come to protect us." That was the general feeling of most of the benighted people in the Near East toward Americans in those days. Maybe they still feel that way. Uncle Sam is a true friend of the "under-dog."

When we arrived at the landing, they greeted us with open arms, but we quickly got into the motor cars and started for the distant farm of the Dilboys. It was a clearing on the top of a hill from which we could see the little *Litchfield* at anchor in the bay.

It was not easy to win over the mother of Dilboy but his father was not long in seeing our side of it. The poor man never got over the fact that the President of the United States sent him a monthly check for fifty dollars to express the nation's gratitude for the service of his son. No one had explained that his son had taken out government insurance. But the mother wept and kept gazing down upon the bay where her boy lay beneath the flag of his adopted country. Finally she agreed and pleaded tearfully through the interpreter: "Take care of my boy."

Months later, a friend sent me a clipping from a Washington paper. It told of the Chesme boy's military funeral at Arlington, with the Dilboy Post of the American Legion in charge. It was evidently an impressive ceremony. We all felt that the bugler's taps on that day and the reverent hand salutes of his old "buddies" brought a fitting end to the career of the young Greek-American who had offered his life for his friends.

CHAPTER 20

A Visit to Almeria

THE spring schedule of the European squadron had sent our destroyer, the *McCormick*, skirting the north shores of the Mediterranean. We spent many happy days at Naples and then at Leghorn where we visited the Italian Naval Academy. We enjoyed the hospitality of Genoa and the Mardi Gras jollities of Nice. At Barcelona we attended a gala bull fight. Now again we were at sea, bent on "showing the flag" to the cities that lay peacefully on the eastern coast of Spain. We steamed southward from Barcelona at twenty knots, taking head seas green over the bow, whereupon the grim little fighter staged its spectacular imitation of a bucking broncho. And let it be said here that many a salty officer and man of our division, after years of service in the destroyer flotillas, suffered from the mysterious unpleasantness of *mal de mer* quite as much as the tourist on his first ocean trip. Only the going is infinitely more trying in a destroyer. That winter we rolled forty degrees on a passage from Athens to Malta.

From the navigating bridge we studied the ever-changing vista of mountain ridges and their ancient Moorish look-out towers—those everlasting souvenirs of an era as war-cursed as our own. But the Spain we visited then was enjoying a happy escape from the misery of the first

World War. There was still a king on his throne and there was no sign of impending civil strife.

Our naval mission at the time was to assist at Cartagena at the ceremony of laying a wreath at the monument erected to the memory of the soldiers and sailors who gave their lives in Cuba and the Philippines during the Spanish-American War. The American admiral in command of the European squadron had offered thus to honor the Spanish heroes.

Church and State stood together on that verdant morning in May to acknowledge the patriotism of those sons of Spain who once had ventured far overseas in her ships of war. The church authorities invited me to bless the monument.

A lively crowd of civilians joined the soldiers and sailors of the United States and Spain in attendance at the ceremony of laying the wreath. Passing years had swept away all traces of ill feeling. Elderly naval and military officers, vested now in that quiet dignity which is born of a matured sense of the futility of human hates, joined hearts at the foot of that marble shaft. The Spanish captain-general, a bearded old gentleman, imperial in a profusion of gold braid, delivered a fiery eulogy for the heroic dead, and he lauded too the American Navy for its courteous tribute. His aide-de-camp, an elderly and stalwart soldier, stood beside him. It was he who at the luncheon that day in the home of the captain-general jokingly told us that he was among those captured by Dewey's fleet at the battle of Manila Bay. He said that he remembered it all vividly, that he had not been treated unkindly. It was interesting to be a guest under such circumstances.

They lent me a precious lace surplice and an old and

rich cope which they had brought over from the cathedral. Several of the local clergy took part in the ceremony. It was impressive and important, but I believe that the visit of the "Little Sisters of the Poor" to our destroyer, *McCormick*, will always be remembered as the really high light of our stay at Almeria. It happened in this way.

The morning after we arrived I stood on the forecastle chatting with Jim Haggerty, the ship's leading gunner's mate. Jim was a young petty officer and hard as a "holy stone," the stroke oar of our race-boat crew, and a splendid seaman. It was an odd coincidence that he should be telling me then of his sister in Philadelphia who had recently taken the veil as a Sister of Charity. But he was not the only sailor in the crew who could boast of having a nun in the family. As it turned out we discovered that the destroyer *McCormick* had five sailors who enjoyed that distinction.

As Jim and I stood there looking across the Bay of Almeria we both saw at the same moment an approaching whaleboat. It was obviously standing toward our ship.

"Looks like they're headin' this way, Father," said Haggerty. "Guess I'd better tell the officer of the deck." Jim hurried aft to the gangway.

The whaleboat flew the Spanish ensign of red and gold, and the oars were manned by sailors of the Royal Navy. It struck me that this must indeed be a visit of importance. My binoculars then revealed two little nuns seated on an after thwart near the coxswain.

They passed the word of their coming to our commanding officer who was below in his cabin. He hurried up the ladder, and reached the welldeck just as the whaleboat came alongside. The gentle nuns, in their austere habits, slowly climbed aboard. You might have heard a pin drop on the steel deck as the American sailors waited for their arrival on the top grating of the gangway. A bit out of breath, perhaps, and a little shy, they smiled as they stepped aboard. One of the nuns, the older one of the two, was unmistakably Spanish, and we soon discovered that she was old enough to be feeble. She spoke no English. Her companion, a young Irish nun, full of the spirit of youth, acted as interpreter.

They were "Little Sisters of the Poor," and they came to beg for their old paupers who dwelt in the "Asilio" on the hill overlooking the city of Almeria. The Irish nun pointed it out to us as we grouped near the torpedo tubes. It was not so much money they wanted as food: sugar, coffee, and especially canned fruits. This was expensive in town, they said, and "the old men like it; it is good for them." Fortunately it was not money they wanted, for we hadn't seen the paymaster for months. What funds we had drawn from the books had been spent sightseeing in the cities of the north.

The captain sent for the commissary steward and told him what to do. By this time several of the deck force came aft to greet the Sisters. They said they were so sorry to be "broke," but they felt, however, something might be done to help them out. While the captain spoke with the Spanish nun, Jim Haggerty captured the attention of her Irish companion. I knew that Jim was telling the little nun about his "kid sister" who had recently become a religious in Philadelphia.

We officers invited the Sisters to the wardroom where, we explained, it would be more comfortable than on topside, standing on deck, exposed to the cold winds. But no, they must leave presently as they felt it unwise to detain the Spanish sailors any longer than was necessary. It occurred to me they found it far more interesting to chat with the bluejackets.

My notes record that Otto Lang, the chief commissary steward, filled three sacks with twenty-four pounds of coffee, several pounds of sugar, butter and many tins of preserved peaches and pears and figs. The Spanish sailors below in the whaleboat nudged one another when our sailors lugged the sacks down the gangway and placed them in the bottom of the boat. The nuns were delightfully appreciative.

As they stepped over the side, they thanked the captain, and promised to pray for us. A few minutes later they waved a cheery farewell, as the oars of the Spanish seamen swept them across the white-capped Bay of Almeria.

That evening at dusk, as we stood out to sea, I rather felt that many eyes of the crew were focussed on that white "Asilio" on the hill beyond Almeria. Some of us knew that it was the hour of evening prayer.

CHAPTER 21

Sky Pilot

RETURNING from the European station in June, 1924, the sea was rough and life hard to endure. We had looked forward to a swift crossing in the destroyer *McCormick* but head winds and heavy seas made us put in at Ponta del Garda in the Azores for fuel. From then on we struggled against grim opposition; some days we made only five knots against seas that loomed twenty feet above the bridge and made us feel alone by shutting from view the other ships of the division. Only thoughts of New York and family reunions sustained our spirits. It interested me to note that most of the sailors intended, on their first afternoon ashore, to see a big league game. They had been in Europe for over two years. Yankee Stadium symbolized the home land.

After spending a leave with my sister Anita's family at Newport, Rhode Island, and with father in Bethlehem, Pennsylvania, orders for duty on the staff of the Commander of Aircraft Squadrons, Battle Force, sent me across the continent to San Diego, California.

The day I arrived to relieve Father George Murdock, a naval aviator lost his life. The tragic aftermath kept the chaplain busy well into the night. I learned that it was an era of plane crashes. Aviation was still in the hands of intrepid pioneers and the tools they worked with were none too satisfactory.

In those days, although the force had two tenders, the *Aroostook* and the *Gannet*, the unmarried aviators lived on North Island in the batchelor officers' quarters, known simply as B.O.Q. I was assigned a room there and I fast got to know the bird-men and to admire their skill and daring and genuine camaraderie. My vocabulary soon gained new terms that lifted my interest in the Navy literally from the ship's deck to the skies.

"Tex" Weller, an officer pilot of Fighting Squadron Two, gave me my first stunt hop. In the front seat of a Vought, I "got the works" in the form of loops and Immelmann turns, but I promised "Tex" I would be back for more. Destroyer life in the Black Sea, when it became especially "black," had schooled me in acrobatics.

The pilots and the sailors who flew with them knew the limitations of their planes. In the mess they told of mechanical failures and forced landings. They felt that the Navy was slow in grasping the value of aviation; and this impelled many to advocate a separate air force under an independent command. The commander of the aircraft squadrons, Captain Stanford E. Moses, sensed this disturbing attitude and worked hard to indoctrinate the officers regarding the Navy's fixed stand. But it was only after Captain Joseph M. Reeves assumed command that all hands became convinced that the American system of welding Navy and Aviation was the answer. It was his thorough mastery of the philosophy of naval warfare and his eloquence that won the day. Every week he lectured to all the squadron officers and pointed out the fallacy of a separate air force. The British Navy today rues the hour they set a course in the other direction.

My aviator friends, in those hard times of the middle twenties, made a lasting impression on my mind because they were highly individualistic—more so, perhaps, than my former shipmates in the Fleet. The younger pilots, naturally, served in the fighting squadrons. Their mission required the quick facility of young nerves. They flew small, fast planes which seemed to step up the tempo of their personalities.

I recall a flight with Lieutenant "Jimmie" E. Dyer who later received the Schiff Trophy from President Coolidge. Jimmie's plane was a speedy little fighter, but one day he offered me a hop and a flying lesson in another machine, an old "Jenny." He acted like an impatient traveller who by some stroke of ill luck was forced to ride a freight train. Jimmie, a bit older now, is a "big boat" skipper, lately returned from the Asiatic Fleet where he commanded a squadron.

Whenever a pilot was killed in a crash, and crashes were numerous in those days, the chaplain was expected to be the first to carry the news to his widow. The most harrowing task I have ever undertaken was on the morning seven of our men were killed when a big flying boat plunged into the sea off Coronado. In order to reach the families of the victims before sympathetic friends unwisely telephoned, I sped to homes in Coronado and San Diego, breaking the frightful news. Fortunately I had developed the technique of having navy women of the neighborhood, whom I had first notified, stand by to take charge after I had delivered the dreadful message.

Never shall I forget the mistake I made one morning when I drove with a fellow officer to Coronado to ask Eva Dyer, the wife of my friend Jimmie, how many chairs would be needed for the bridge party she was promoting for the benefit of St. Mary's Hospital. We drove to the Dyer home and stepped from the car when Eva, who had seen us through the window of the living room, dashed to the front porch crying hysterically, "Oh! Jim's been killed!" I knew Eva to be among the most courageous of the squadron wives. This taught me a lesson. From that day I never drove in the streets of Coronado until the last plane was safe in the hangar. Visiting a home during the day had but one meaning.

But life in the air squadrons was not so unpleasant as this story may indicate. The patience and courage of the aviators' wives was so fine that the morale of the pilots was exceptionally high. Dinner parties were numerous and gay. One feels something of the atmosphere of wartime when men live dangerously, sustained by the loving encouragement of their wives. It struck me in those days that every time a pilot took off, he flew over the enemy's lines—the enemy of faulty motors, wings and struts.

One afternoon I stood on the flight deck of the *Langley* and saw Lieutenant Jack Tate make a perfect landing but one of the struts carried away in a cloud of dry rot. That plane was a "crate" and the infuriated Jack was quick to say so, "My God! They make us fly those things!"

When the Navy Yard installed new flag quarters in the *Langley* the force commander and his official family moved aboard. Captain Reeves to whom we gave (as is the custom) the courtesy title of "commodore," asked me to organize and run the officers' mess. The steward was a good cook and did especially well whenever Commander Karl Smith sent us wild ducks he had shot in the lake country. One of the jolliest dinner parties I have ever given was the night I invited Father George O'Meara and the Walter Fitches to dinner on board the old *Langley*. Father O'Meara had volunteered his services as the first Catholic chaplain at the naval training station and worked among recruits for over two years. I shall always appreciate his influence on my work. As president of St. Augustine's Preparatory School in San Diego he was an expert mentor of young men. A few years later he became chaplain of the San Quentin prison and for the past fifteen years has continued his priestly ministration among the less fortunate. Now a cheerful philosopher and friend of discouraged men, Father O'Meara is the most tolerant and successful chaplain I have ever known. Although he now is the rector of a large parish in San Raphael, California, he spends his mornings in the prison and calls daily on those condemned to the lethal chamber.

The *Langley* was our first plane carrier; a slow moving, converted collier with a roof on it, where our fliers learned to land their planes on the rolling and pitching deck. The sailors called her the "Covered Wagon." Nowadays carriers steam fast into the wind, and the planes are vastly superior. I recall landing on the *Langley's* deck with Lieutenant Andy Krinkley; and I still wonder at his skill. The flight deck really looked no larger than a three-cent stamp when he "nosed her down" for the landing.

The chief engineer of the *Langley* was Lieutenant Charles J. Rend, an old friend of my earliest days in the service. One night on the landing, I ran across Charlie when he was on his way from Brest to Paris to propose to Helen Diemer, a student at the Sorbonne; I went to their marriage in San Francisco and baptized their first child in San Diego. I have always felt close to the Rends. Charlie is now in command of the smart destroyer *Balch*, operating in Hawaiian waters.

When the air squadron sailed on fleet maneuvers in the spring of 1925 I took passage in the *Aroostook*. She was once a Fall River boat, converted during the World War into a mine-layer and then into an airplane tender. She was a fine ship and a happy home even though the men called her the "Beeno." When I first heard the word I wondered if it were a strange term in the new science of flying. Then they told me how the *Aroostook* got her nickname. One evening, while moored at North Island, the crew had an emergency task of taking on stores and fuel for a cruise. The bosun's mate gruffly passed the word: "There'll *be no* liberty tonight." Later he again shouted: "There'll *be no* movies." From that moment she became the "Beeno" ship. In spite of the strenuous efforts of her efficient skipper, Commander Wilbur R. Van Auken, she remained the "Beeno" as long as I was in her.

That summer, when the rest of the Fleet made a cruise to Australia, Fleet Air remained in Hawaii. The reason, perhaps, was to assist Commander John Rodgers on his non-stop flight to the Islands. The *Aroostook* went on the ten-day search for the lost plane. I shall not forget the experience because I, for several days, stood a heel and toe watch as a "look-see boy" on the flying bridge.

In the *Langley* when the ship was at sea, I had many interesting talks with Commander John H. Towers, who was then the executive officer. He is now a rear admiral and chief of the Bureau of Aeronautics. He told of the days when, as one of the Navy's first fliers, he got his flight training in the frail and primitive machines then in use. One of his stories had a strange and pathetic twist. He told of a flight over the water near Annapolis when his plane fell apart in mid-air and crashed. He said that every bone in his body was bruised or broken, but he managed to cling to the wreckage until long after the sun went down. When he felt he could hold on no longer, he heard in the dark the sound of a motor and the barking of a dog. The dog continued to bark as the boat reached him and the crew hauled him aboard. The little dog in the bow was his pet.

I heard a great deal about naval aviation in the flag mess of the *Langley*. The commodore, who later became a four-star admiral and commander-in-chief of the Fleet, spoke brilliantly with the clearness and conviction of a distinguished professor; and he had a fine sense of humor. One of his favorite stories was of a young student who in off hours had developed a talent for the stage by taking small parts in road shows that came to the college town. One day, growing weary of carrying a spear, he asked for a speaking part. He vowed he would convince the local public of his histrionic ability. They gave him just one line in the funeral scene of the second act. It was simply: "Stand back! and let the coffin pass."

He rehearsed it strenuously. He repeated the line endlessly, each time stressing a different word to improve the effect. On the night of his first appearance, still muttering to himself the precious words, his great moment finally came. With a slight shudder and a nervous sweep of his hand, he exclaimed: "Stand back! And let the parson cough!"

The days were full of life in Fleet Air.

CHAPTER 22

Rendezvous in the Sun

AT RISK of breaking the sequence of this narrative I must tell a bit more of life with the air squadrons at San Diego.

Whenever Lieutenant "Greek" Garrett crossed the length of the great lounge room of bachelor officers' quarters you felt he had been an athlete in his midshipmen days. In spite of long tours of sea duty in small ships and big, he had kept himself fit. He now was a peacetime ace in naval aviation. Garrett and his best friend, "Bubbles" Fisher, were the first aviators I met when I joined the air squadrons at San Diego, California. You still hear amusing anecdotes about those two young naval officers. Each had a distinct and well-defined personality, and a keen sense of fun, although they chose individual forms of expression. I can still see hundreds of aviation "mechs" at the noon hour walking from the hangars to the mess hall with their heads craned toward the sky, their faces wrinkled in smiles, while "Bubbles" Fisher in his single-seater flew above them upside down. No one was surprised to learn that Fisher, when his plane once crashed eleven miles off the coast, swam to the beach and lived to tell what a job it was to convince the family, living in a beach shack, that he was sane. He was naked and undoubtedly the image of a mad caveman. Fisher played a marvelous game of end on the Fleet Air football team which "Greek" Garrett organized and coached. From the start I grew fond of both men. But this anecdote is mostly about "Greek."

Garrett was universally popular, winning friends in a much less spectacular way than Fisher. His sunny, intelligent face still haunts the mind's eye of those who served with him in the middle twenties. When "Greek" entered the messroom you naturally dropped your paper, looked up and waited for him to talk, wondering whether you would have an apt retort to his inevitable "gag."

In those days aviation was more a sport than it is now. There were fewer restrictions. It was commonplace to hear of a shipmate zooming up a Santa Fé train to frighten the passengers as they lumbered over the rails toward Los Angeles. "Greek" was not a devotee of this sort of acrobatics. Nor was his D H plane suitable for stunts.

Coaching the air squadrons' football team was "extra duty" and a painful chore, for "Greek" knew that he was expected to play halfback on the sailors' team and spearhead most of the offensive play. But he bore up under it cheerfully. Looking back over the years, I believe our interest was mostly in Garrett rather than in the outcome of the game. We cheered because we wanted him to win. Although it was years since he had played at the Naval Academy, his game was still a joy to look upon. One caught the vivid spark of his leadership. The way the bluejackets blocked for him on his runs around end thrilled us. Then afterward, bruised from head to foot, Greek limped to the dinner table and braved the quips of his messmates with a grin on his weather-lined face.

Cross-country hops were considered then rather a privilege than a necessity. Aviators complained about the attitude of the high command. The reason may have been that motors were inferior and that emergency landing fields were few and hard to find.

After a trying day in the air, "Greek" Garrett often came to my room in b.o.q., tossed his cap on the dresser, stretched out on the bed and thought aloud. "They've got to improve those 'crates,' padre. No wonder they call our D H's 'flying coffins.' On a poor landing they're apt to explode in your face. Some day they'll give us air-cooled jobs. Those things we're flyin' now are bad news." He would lie there in his khaki and boots, dog-tired, a little discouraged, but still hopeful of better planes and happier landings. At times he would doze, and I would have to rouse him when the Filipino mess attendant came by the door, striking his gong as summons to dinner.

One day I requested authority of the force commander to ask a pilot to fly me to San Pedro where Father Joseph Casey was holding a mission for the Fleet. I asked "Greek" if he wanted the assignment. He was delighted. But later in the day he told me that his section of the squadron had been ordered to fly to Yuma, Arizona, with himself in command. So I asked Lieutenant Earl Wilkins to fly me north instead.

The next morning at dawn I heard the powerful "Liberty Motors" warming up and then the great roar of the collective take-off. I peered out the window as the six planes completed their first encirclement of the field and headed individually for the foothills beyond La Mesa. As they passed over San Diego they effected a closer formation and steadily climbed in the half light of dawn for a high crossing of the Sierra Madre.

On our return that evening in the Vought we taxied up to a hangar and discovered a "mech" running toward us and shouting something to Wilkins. The din of the whirling propeller made too great a barrier to hear his yell of anguish. But I noticed that the pilot's head drooped as he sat there in silence. In an instant he tore off his helmet, struggled out of his parachute and turned his tear-dimmed eyes to me. "Greek Garrett's been killed," he moaned, "at Yuma." I felt as though struck in the face.

We swung to the ground and walked slowly to the hangar. It was not until "Greek's" wingmates returned from Yuma that we learned he had died to save another. In order to avoid crashing into a less skillful pilot who blundered in landing, "Greek" had pulled up, lost flying speed—and crashed. The tanks of his D H exploded at the impact. He and his "mech" had no chance to escape.

Wilkins and I went to my room where others joined us. Never before or since have I seen strong and fearless men so shaken by tragedy. They loved "Greek" Garrett.

That evening, alone in my room, I strove to become realistic in face of what was to come. The book of naval regulations told how to proceed with the details of the funeral. After services in the station chapel the remains would be escorted by all hands to Spanish Bight, where the bridge crosses over to Coronado. From there Garrett's body would be taken to his home in the north. Then the band would head again toward the hangars and try to cheer us with a tune played in quick tempo; and officers and men would proceed to the planes and the air. I kept asking myself, "What about the eulogy?" I paced the floor for hours on a quest for words that might be worthy of the beloved "Greek." It must be brief, I thought. It must articulate the feelings of those who knew him so intimately well—fearless men whose hearts had not hardened with their nerves.

Thoughts came jumbled like the débris of a wreck. In despair I donned my blouse and cap and went through the passageways of the quarters, looking for the squadron commander, Millington McComb, my old friend of the *Florence H.* disaster. I found him in the lounge with "Bubbles" Fisher who had been taking an inventory of "Greek's" personal effects. In the files was a letter requesting that Fisher be given that heart-breaking task. I told "Mac" what I needed: a fact, or a remark, perhaps, that "Greek" may have made before the last take-off, or an incident of their midshipman days at Annapolis—anything to portray the sort of man he was.

Commander McComb lighted a cigarette. "I have it. Just before the take-off 'Greek' got his pilots together, and pointing to the bright glow over the hills in the East, he said, 'Fellows, we'll rendezvous in the sun. Let's go.' Those were his last words."

It was characteristic of "Greek" to choose the sun for his last rendezvous. All his life he had sought sunlight for his friends and, finding it, he gave it away.

CHAPTER 23

New York

SOME TIME later I received orders to the transport, *Chaumont*, for passage through the Panama Canal to Norfolk, Virginia. The orders also stated that I should further report to the commandant of the Navy Yard, New York. Father Raymond Drinan relieved me of my duties in the air squadrons. It was the beginning of a cycle, for years later I followed him to the Asiatic Fleet; recently he took over my duties at the training station in San Diego, California.

While looking for the place assigned me in the mess room of the *Chaumont*, I discovered an officer standing beside me whose face looked familiar. He turned to me with a smile and asked, "Aren't you 'Macaroni Maguire'?" Then I knew that the many warm sea-days ahead would not be tedious.

My neighbor was Lieutenant Commander DeWitt C. "Pete" Emerson of the dental corps. His reference to macaroni recalled the day we had hastily met as I was leaving the little restaurant that Caesar ran on a side street in Tia Juana, Mexico. That afternoon, for the sake of variety, four of us Fleet Air people motored across the border to Caesar's place for dinner. Also, for the same reason, I asked Caesar whether he could bake macaroni the way mother prepared it when I was a boy in Elmira.

Caesar jubilantly led me to the galley, where, hampered by my uncertain coaching, he cooked a big bowl of macaroni, baked with parmesan cheese, and glorified with an exquisite sauce. When he had placed it on the table, he made a little speech: "Gentlemen, I hope you will enjoy the padre's masterpiece. I christen it, 'Macaroni Maguire.'" It was good, but I never dreamed the name would survive. Dr. Emerson said he had often ordered it for his friends. That may have explained why we became companions in the *Chaumont*, and later shared a large apartment in the St. George Hotel in Brooklyn. I saw "Pete" the other day in the dispensary at Pearl Harbor, Hawaii; he was wearing four stripes on his shoulder marks as a newly-commissioned captain in the dental corps.

The day I reported at the Brooklyn Navy Yard, I went to the naval hospital to call on my esteemed predecessor, Father Matthew Gleeson. He was sunning himself on a bench near the hospital gate. In his soothing Irish brogue, he said: "William, me b'y, I'm glad to see you." The grand old padre, having come to the end of a twenty-year cruise in the Navy, was tired. He had been our first fleet chaplain. It gave me especial pride in my new assignment to be Father Gleeson's relief and his father confessor the last year of his priestly life.

For ten years, wherever I had served, the older officers had asked me, "Do you know Padre Gleeson?" Then, they usually told a story about him. Twenty years ago at a dinner dance on board the battleship *New Mexico*, the commanding officer, Captain Arthur Willard, asked me the usual question, and spun the following yarn: One day, on a cruise, when they were young shipmates, Willard was officer of the deck, and while admonishing a blundering sailor, his temper got out of hand and he used an assortment of fiery terms of the sea, until he noticed Father Gleeson standing near by, within hearing. Later in reply to Willard's apology, the padre said, "Arthur, me b'y, I was thinking I might write His Holiness, the Pope, and ask him to make you his special procurator for profanity."

The night before Father Gleeson died, I was summoned on an emergency call to the hospital. When leaving at three in the morning, I saw a light in his room. I peered through the open door and found him awake. Seeing me, he said, "Come in, William, me b'y, I was just chuckling over a story Mike McGonnigle, an old shipmate, told me today. Sit down, and I'll tell it to you."

This was Father Gleeson's last story. It is a pity I cannot repeat it in his own priceless way.

It seems that McGonnigle, a "mustang" lieutenant, who had lost none of the rough edges acquired as an enlisted man, was in command of a barracks during World War I at Queenstown, Ireland. With the signing of the armistice came orders to police the barracks thoroughly and make it shipshape for the British when they came to take over. McGonnigle personally supervised the last "field-day" his men held at the place, and gave them a "well done." Then he waited for the British army officer to relieve him of his command. Finally, a swank major, boasting a monocle and a swagger stick, came to McGonnigle's office. Concealing his aversion to foppery, the naval lieutenant offered to show the Englishman through the barracks. He was proud to reveal how well his men had done with bucket and brush. After the inspection, the Englishman said, "Well, old top, the only thing left to do is to fumigate the place." McGonnigle was thunder-struck. "Fumigate! Where d'ya get that stuff!" The major, removing his monocle, replied, "Oh, we'll buy it at the chemist's." Father Gleeson had shared the woes of his shipmates, but he allowed humor to triumph in the end.

One day, years ago, in the battleship *Maine*, Lieutenant Commander Max Mike Frucht said to me, "Padre, you ought to study the methods of Father Gleeson." When pressed for details he continued, "As a young ensign years ago I reported on board the cruiser *New York* in Manila. Father Gleeson met me at the gangway. Although I had never seen him before, he greeted me like a shipwrecked sailor. 'Hello, Max, me b'y. I'm glad to see you. The admiral told me to look out for you.' Then he took me below and introduced me to my new shipmates. The next day my wife came out to the ship to dinner. In the passageway, heading for the wardroom, we ran across Father Gleeson. He put out his hand and said, 'Why, Susan, fancy seeing you out here!' That made a lasting impression. Father Gleeson knew everyone's first name; and he made you feel you had known him all your life."

My colleague at the Navy Yard whom I liked to call "my curate," was the beloved Stanton W. Salisbury, a staunch Presbyterian. We worked in approved navy style, visiting the hospital wards together, rounding up the men of our respective faiths and turning over to each other cases that required our special ministration. We had adjoining offices in a building next to the brig and we shared the same yeoman. We went together in our "boiled shirts" to official dinners in New York, and we were so often found in each other's company that civilians were amazed over this unusual sort of teamwork.

One night, in navy dinner dress we accompanied Admiral "Cy" Plunkett and his staff to a reception in Mecca Temple in honor of Evangeline Booth. The Secretary of the Navy, Mr. Curtis Wilbur, was there. I sat beside a colorful seagoing captain whose nickname was "Juggy." We were seated on the stage in the second row of officers. In front of me was the admiral. I could easily see, when the tambourine was being passed for some worthy cause, that the admiral had taken a dollar bill from his pocket. Not wanting to outdo the "old man," I reached in my pocket for a bill of the same modest value. But I drew out a fiver and quickly put it back; trying again until I extracted a bill of the desired importance. "Juggy" saw the five-dollar bill in my hand but failed to observe my final movements. Not wanting to be outdone, "Juggy" rumpled a fiver in his freckled fist and waited for the tambourine. When he saw me drop what the boys call a "frog skin," he nearly fainted; but it was too late. I dare not quote him for fear I might do an injustice to his salty vocabulary.

Only once did I regret that I was a "shipmate" of Salisbury. It was when we were giving a course of "pep talks" to the hospital corpsmen. The commanding officer had asked us to speak to his men on alternate Tuesdays. In order to catch their attention I usually told them the latest story I had picked up among my friends in New York. But my stories never quite "jelled." Holding back my own giggles over a yarn I thought really funny, they sat with "dead pan" expressions. One day I confided in Salisbury my feeling of utter failure as a wit and found out that as I had always tried out the new story on Stanton he, having a week's headstart, had passed it on to the corpsmen! On hearing me repeat the yarn they were definitely not amused.

Our job also had to do with interviewing deserters. They came to us in the hope of gaining a recommendation for clemency. At times we luckily discovered a reason why a man should not be sent to the naval prison for having taken "French leave." One day a man came to the office with a pathetic tale of grief. A few years before he had deserted from the naval air station at Pensacola, Florida. During the first year of his enlistment there, he had earned extra compensation as a barber. He had saved his money and married. One day, when they decided to send all such "politicians" to sea, the barber, fearing financial hardship, "went over the hill." In New York he got a job in the barber shop of the Racquet and Tennis Club, and did well until the Douglas Robinson, the Assistant Secretary of the Navy, chose him as his favorite barber. On Monday mornings when the Secretary came for a shave, he invariably told the barber about the Navy and how loyal, industrious and faithful the sailors were. He even suggested that the barber enlist. The strain on the poor fellow's conscience became unbearable. He examined his bank book and decided that while he was in the Portsmouth naval prison there would be enough money to support his wife and child. He came to the Yard and turned himself in.

While listening to his story, a thought struck me. I recalled that Duncan Harris was one of the governors of the Racquet Club. I phoned him and suggested that he ask Mr. Robinson to do something for his favorite barber.

I felt the lad was already rehabilitated. That night a dispatch came from the office of the Secretary of the Navy granting the deserter a "special order discharge" from the service. From then on, Mondays, for the club barber, ceased to be "blue."

From childhood days in Elmira, when father gave us a punching bag and gloves and taught us the rudiments, boxing, as a sport, always impressed me as being correctly named the manly art of self-defense. Like every other human activity it can be overemphasized and carried beyond the original purpose of its invention; but in its place, I had found the sport especially wholesome for navy men. Years ago in China, I wrote an editorial in the *Asiatic Four Stacker*, the squadron weekly, in which I drew an analogy between boxing and making a liberty. A man in the ring is on his own, fortified only by what he knows of the sport, his strength, courage and will to win. A man "leading with his chin" on a liberty in town is like the man who stupidly lowers his guard in the boxing ring.

Boxing, in the Navy, trains men in the virtues of self-discipline, perseverance and fairness. It strengthens the character of the man-o'-war's man. The most successful boxers I have known in ships were modest, upright, and good sports. My friend, Joe Fisher, now a chief bosun's mate, long held the All-Navy lightweight championship. In his fighting days Joe would chase his handlers from the dressing room just before he entered the ring. When he was alone, he dropped to his knees and prayed. It interested me to know what sort of a petition Joe made when he prayed, and I asked him to tell me one night after he had whipped the champion of the west coast. Joe replied,

"I pray that I won't hurt the other fellow, and that I may win the bout fair and square."

It delighted me while in New York to be able to stage navy smokers in a big machine shop in the Yard. We matched the sailors from various ships that were there for overhaul and offered simple prizes to the winners. It became a popular diversion and gave the men a more wholesome interest than the usual attractions of a big city. I was especially fortunate that my cousin, John P. Maguire, was a director of Madison Square Garden, and my brother, Walter, was the managing engineer of that huge establishment. It was through them that the sailors of the Navy Yard met such celebrities as "Tex" Rickard, Tommy Loughran, and Jack Sharkey. They came to the Yard and refereed the bouts. Rickard usually made a graceful speech in praise of navy sportsmanship. One night Sharkey told the men of the day he walked across the Brooklyn Bridge with nothing in his pocket but thirteen cents and the address of the Sands Street recruiting office. He told the big audience of sailors that a cruise in the Fleet and clean living afloat had been responsible for his rise to fame and fortune.

One night, with truckloads of park benches borrowed from Flatbush, and every available mess bench from ships in the Yard, we packed 8,000 fight fans in a machine shop for a gala smoker. The Assistant Secretary of the Navy was a guest of the commandant. Members of the Fourth Estate—John B. Kennedy, Corey Ford, Paul Gallico, who wrote a humorous piece for the *Daily News,* and the editorial staff of *Colliers*—witnessed the excitement from ringside seats. Arthur "Bugs" Baer refereed a comedy bout and stopped the show. Joe Humphries, the famed announcer, assisted me as master of ceremonies and made the steel rafters ring with his inimitable cry at the end of a bout—"The WINNAH-H-H-H-H!"

After the smoker we had Jack Maguire's party and the celebrities on board the cruiser *Seattle* for a supper of navy beans.

On a cold day in November, my old school friend, Lucien B. Coppinger, took me to see the Army-Notre Dame football game. We sat in the grandstand of the Yankee Stadium, bundled up to the ears. Between the halves, when those near us were silently busy with refreshments that warm the heart, I turned to him, not realizing how far my voice could carry, and said, "Cop, I'm going to marry Snelson Chesney's daughter next week in East Orange. You know Chesney. He's in Jack Maguire's bank."

Coppinger took up from there. "Nice going. Have you met his daughter?"

"No. But I expect to meet her at a luncheon next Wednesday at the Waldorf."

At that moment I heard a roar behind me and felt a lusty whack on my soft hat. "Great balls of tar!" yelled a Notre Dame rooter. "What a man! He's marryin' the gal next week, and he hasn't met her yet. Put it there, pal." He grabbed my hand and swung me around so the customers could get a good view of my red face. Being in mufti there was nothing I could do.

That night when Coppinger and I returned to his hotel, I chided him on being so elated over the Notre Dame victory. He said, "I'm not a graduate of Notre Dame, but it makes me feel good when they win. I like the spirit of the 'Fighting Irish.' " I had never realized how many loyal sons of Notre Dame there are in the country until we walked through the corridor to where an old woman was on her knees, scrubbing the deck. Evidently she heard the words, "Fighting Irish." She raised her head as we passed and smiled, "Ain't it grand they won." Every Irishman in the country, though he never got out of the third grade, calls Notre Dame his alma mater.

In August, 1927, Father Gleeson died. Officers and men of the Navy and civilians from the city attended the solemn Requiem Mass at St. Patrick's Cathedral. His eminence, Cardinal Hayes presided. Monsignor Chidwick, a hero of the *Maine*, delivered the eulogy. Many navy chaplains came from afar to pay a last tribute to their beloved colleague. They marched in the funeral cortege on Fifth Avenue and stood beside me when I read the last prayers at Father Gleeson's grave.

Although this account of my tour of duty in New York is mostly about the fun I had, much of my time was devoted to the patients in the hospital, helping the sick and dying, offering the consolation that only religion can give. I still felt though, that a navy chaplain's proper place is in the Fleet. With the aid of Chaplain Curtis H. Dickens, our chief in the bureau, I obtained orders to the battleship *Arkansas*, which was then fitting out in Philadelphia, for a cruise in the Caribbean Sea.

CHAPTER 24

A Cruise in the Arkansas

L IFE in the battleship, *Arkansas*, gave me a sea change I heartily welcomed. The officers and men had ship-spirit pitched to a high degree. The ship's company attacked every mission like a football squad making its first dashing entry upon the field. The high command in those days encouraged competitive ambitions among the units of the Fleet covering the wide area of gunnery, engineering, communications, and sports. We were so busy (and the Navy has not changed) that the days came and vanished like the wind.

A few days after I had joined the ship in Philadelphia we got up anchor for Guantanamo Bay, Cuba, a naval base acquired after the Spanish-American War. We steamed down the Delaware through cakes of ice, but in a few days we were in our white uniforms enjoying movies on topside and sleeping under the stars. I offered daily Mass in the crew's reception room and began the long day immediately after quarters for muster.

My first task was to revive the ship's weekly paper, called the *Arklight*. My close friend and shoregoing companion, Lieutenant A. Finley France, in spite of the fact that he was assistant gunnery officer and officer in charge of athletics, offered to be an associate editor. The first number of the *Arklight* was published in the nature of a "gag." It was a dummy run having only headlines above blank columns and an editorial admonition to the effect that the ship's paper would continue to look like that unless all hands turned to and gave us suitable copy.

France asked me one day, when they were shorthanded, to be a torpedo observer in a force battle practice. There was no doubt in my mind that I saw from the foretop, where I stood, that the "*Arkie*" had been hit by three torpedoes, fired by the "enemy" destroyers. I made the report. It affected me as much as it did "Fin" because it lowered the ship's score. The next time he decided to employ one whose eyesight might not be quite so accurate.

If I were to enumerate all the jobs that were given me in the *Arkansas*, one might wonder whether it is a chaplain's "pidgin" to devote so much time to collateral duties. It struck me that it was befitting that I should be entertainment officer in charge of the movies, smokers, Happy Hours, ship's dances in town, stage productions and sightseeing parties. When Finley France was detached I was given his job as assistant athletic officer. The executive officer, Commander John T. G. Stapler, was technically officer in charge of athletics but he delegated his assistant to handle the details. As educational officer I was in charge of the ship's school. I found the routine stimulating because it brought me close to the men. That is the only reason I did not object to going "all out" for the ship.

I worked much harder in those days than I ever did as a harassed curate in Jersey City. But for days running the paper-work enslaved me below decks where I found little evidence that we were actually cruising in the tropic sea.

We spent our week end and upkeep periods anchored in Guantanamo Bay. In company with us were the *Wyoming, Florida,* and *Utah.* We had the best ball team, but our boxers and wrestlers, although as a "stable" they were above average, often ran afoul of better men from the other ships. One of our boxing "prima donnas" was a big fellow called "Bulkhead" Daring. He was heavy-weight champion of the scouting force, and his forte was to crush his opponent with a devastating left-hand swing. His weakness, if that is the word, was lack of speed and the knack of realizing that the other fellow had similar designs upon his own chin. Bulkhead did pretty well in the Fleet, but it was a different story when he accepted "Tex" Rickard's invitation to fight in the "curtain-raisers" in the Garden. The "pros" were a bit too smart for Bulk-head. He usually started brightly, firing magnificent broadsides, following through with an "Admiral's sweep" of his ponderous left. It made a grand impression on the spectators, but that was not the "pay-off." After a round or two of futile swinging, all Bulkhead had left was his good humor. Everyone liked Daring, and hoped he might get along as a professional after his honorable discharge from the Navy. It was agreed he had the size and strength of a "white hope."

While on leave in New York, a few days ago, my cousin, Jack Maguire, said he had settled down and be-come a professional boxer and a member of a millionaire's "stable" on Long Island. Daring was being groomed for a quick rise to the championship of the world. But he had fixed habits that were as strong as his biceps. He confessed that he had been "blitzed" by a "death punch." When asked to explain what he meant, he told, with appropriate gestures, how he had smashed his foe to the ring floor and thought he was "dead," that is unconscious. But the man was not "dead"; he was merely collecting his wits; he rose and threw a punch at Bulkhead that made everything go black. That was a "death punch," delivered by a man supposedly "dead." But it was deadly enough to convince Bulkhead that he should hang up his gloves and ask for a job as a bank guard. The job was his for the asking.

Bulkhead Daring was not the only ex-navy battler to become a bank guard. In the *Arkansas*, Chief Gunner's Mate "Biff" Fitzgerald, was the chief master-at-arms. He told me a story of his early days that had all the gusto of a Hollywood "horse opera." In 1916, Fitzgerald served in a gunboat off the coast of Mexico. The skipper of the ship was, according to the old chief, a "sun-downer," and his ship a "mad-house." He and ten others went "over the hill" and caroused from town to town until they ran across Pancho Villa, the bandit. Fitzgerald and two others signed up as gunnery experts; "Biff" repaired the machine guns. The pay was "d——d" good, and Pancho "made things hum." "Biff" stayed with Villa until the bandit started raiding Texas. This was going too far, even for a navy renegade. One day he told Villa that he was "through," but the Mexican threatened to shoot him if he quit. One night, during a raid, "Biff" made his get-away; crossed the border and turned himself in at a navy recruiting office in New Orleans. I have forgotten how he managed to be reinstated, but the Navy accepted the prodigal and sent him overseas in a destroyer. From then on Fitzgerald made an excellent record. His word was law below decks in the *Arkansas*. At the end of thirty years of service, Fitzgerald came to me and asked if I could find him a job as a bank guard in Boston. That request may have inspired Bulkhead Daring in his choice of a new vocation.

In June, 1928, the *Arkansas* was flagship of the midshipmen's practice squadron. We picked up the midshipmen at Annapolis and took them to Newport on the first leg of the summer cruise. On the passage to Narragansett Bay, a group of midshipmen, led by Edgar J. MacGregor III, came to my room to talk over plans for a musical revue to be staged ashore at Guantanamo Bay. We had several meetings and succeeded, by the time we reached New York, in throwing together a book and assigning parts to our talented shipmates. Influenced by the first syllable of the ship's name, we call the plan "Noah's Nicknacks." MacGregor's father, who had directed several Broadway hits, confided in me, when he took me to lunch at Dinty Moore's, that he feared his son might develop too strong a liking for the stage and quit the Navy. But, out of sheer sportsmanship, he presented us with costumes for the chorus and had a special back-drop painted for the night club scene. We held rehearsals below decks under way; at anchor the bosun's mate passed the word, "Lay aft the actors for the show boat." We piled aboard and then took over the open-air movie theatre at the Guantanamo naval station. A hurricane nearly wrecked the project on the afternoon we held the dress rehearsal. Our most important casualty was the loss of a brand new piano. But we carried on, and staged our performances for the ships of the squadron. I enjoyed working with midshipmen. They were splendid fellows, and they edified the crew by faithfully attending divine services on Sunday.

One day in New York, Corey Ford brought his friend,

Percy Crosby, to the ship for lunch. Crosby saw a copy of the *Arklight* on my desk. He seemed so interested in the little paper that I asked him to make a mast-head, featuring the immortal Skippy. For many months we ran Skippy, sitting under a palm tree, sighting the *Arkansas* through heroic binoculars.

Under the command of Captain Hayne Ellis, the *Arkansas* became what he hoped she would be—"a sweet ship." No skipper ever earned greater loyalty and affection. Our navigator was Commander John F. Shafroth, Jr. Ten years later, we were again shipmates, when he commanded the heavy cruiser *Indianapolis* in the Pacific Fleet. He is now an admiral, serving as Assistant Chief of the Bureau of Navigation.

Another *Arkansas* shipmate, whom I served with in later years, was Lieutenant August J. Detzer, Jr. We were shipmates last year in the *Indianapolis*, serving on the staff of Vice Admiral Adolphus Andrews, Commander, Scouting Force. "Gus," who often spoke of his brother, Karl Detzer, the popular author, is now in command of a destroyer in the Pacific Fleet.

On the cruise to Panama in 1929, Charles Francis Coe, the author, joined us as a guest of the Navy. The jovial "Socker" and I became companions right away and had many pleasant talks about navy life. He had once served as a bluejacket. We stepped ashore in Balboa, while the ship was in one of the locks, to enable Coe to gather material for a novel, before the men of the Fleet should add too many distractions.

When the ship went to Gonaives, Haiti, for a week end, I was given a surprise. The sailor who regularly served at Mass was on watch, and I asked for a volunteer.

An officer in an army uniform arose and said: "Father, may I have the honor of serving Mass?" To my amazement it was Brigadier General Michael Lenihan, U. S. Army. He was on a visit to his daughter, Catherine, whose husband, Lieutenant Paul J. Haloran was on duty in Gonaives. It was years since I had last seen the general. I felt that his courteous gesture that morning was far more effective than my sermon.

CHAPTER 25

The Odessa Portrait

In EARLY June, battleships of the Atlantic Fleet drop anchor about five miles off the shore of Annapolis, Maryland. One can easily view, from the decks, the great dome of the Naval Academy Chapel, nestled in the early summer green of the trees of the Yard. It is the end of "June Week" and hundreds of midshipmen are preparing to embark for the annual practice cruise in European waters. They have welcomed the end of a trying year with its daily routine of drill and study.

To the older officers it is appealing to watch the motor launches, heavily laden with excited youth, pressing onward with their precious cargo. Each midshipman in his uniform of "white works," totes his sea-bag and hammock as he hops from the restless boat to the gangway and climbs the steep ladder to the quarterdeck. He moves with all the restless verve of an explorer at the portals of El Dorado. Although a midshipman is fully aware that a practice cruise is really but a transfer from lectures ashore to lectures and work afloat, with an assortment of ship's drills added for his professional good, he likes the prospects immensely. At least he is in a warship—his world. He soon will learn, in the engine room and on the forecastle, the intricate details of the drama of getting under way. On a summer cruise, he will become familiar with the hundred and one specialties to be mastered for the manning of a modern ship of war. But also he will visit strange ports and meet interesting people at formal dinners and garden parties abroad. He will visit Rome.

Our first evening at sea, as the squadron stood out of the bay in formation, leaving the shores of Virginia and the glow of the west in its churned wake, a young midshipman came over to where I was sitting at the movies. He inquired:

"Father, are we going to see the Pope?"

"Of course, son. One always does."

"Oh, boy. What a break!"

That night the midshipmen heard the boatswain's mate call: "Lights out; keep silence about the decks." They swung into their hammocks in the blue glow of the battle lights and gladly called it a day.

The trans-Atlantic passage that summer was one that gave the young gentlemen a clear conception of the life of those who go down to the sea in ships. For several days we met with furious storms which challenged the might of our steel ships. We "took them over green" until we were off the Cape of Trafalgar, where the navigator, Commander John S. Shaforth, lectured on Nelson's great victory.

Our first port of call was Barcelona, and it took us all of twenty days, what with gunnery drills and ship maneuvering, before we dropped "the hook" in the bay. All hands had many and varied plans for the visit. Some hoped to fly to Madrid; others spoke of a trip to Toledo and Seville, but several hundred had responded to Admiral Harris Laning's radio message in mid-Atlantic, announcing a special Mass that was to be celebrated in one of the larger churches in Barcelona. The admiral had directed that all three ships ascertain the number of officers, midshipmen and sailors who desired to attend the Mass. Over a thousand responded.

Poor Barcelona! How little did her people know what tragedy her future would bring for their beautiful city, on that sunny June morning when our huge church party marched along the wide shaded boulevard with our massed bands playing "Onward Christian Soldiers." We filled the old church of St. Stephen, and I celebrated Solemn High Mass, assisted by distinguished pastors of the city. A young Jesuit priest came over from the Astronomical Observatory and delivered an excellent sermon. He had taught at St. Louis University, and his command of English was extraordinary. He welcomed us "home." He said, "I am sure you must feel at home wherever you assist at Holy Mass."

In Barcelona sightseeing parties for the embryo officers were the order of the day. One rainy afternoon, an agent from one of the tourist bureaus came aboard and I had the mess boy serve us tea in my room. The man interested me.

He was a formidable-looking fellow, tall and broad of shoulder. His blond hair was cropped like a brush, and his blue eyes gave light to a large, expressive face that was unmistakably Russian. On the breast of his blue blouse lay two rows or ribbons, each ribbon representing the national colors of a country whose language this man could speak. He told me that he was an exile from Russia, that he had fought for the Czar in the first World War, and now in addition to his duties as a tour agent, he wrote as an art critic for a magazine published in Latvia.

"Could you tell me something of Brunellov?" I asked.

"Brunellov," he replied, "was a court painter, well known in Russia about seventy-five years ago."

"And tell me, please, who was Kukolnik?" My interest in Russian art seemed to amaze him.

"Kukolnik," he smiled, "was a favorite novelist at the imperial court and a contemporary and bosom friend of Brunellov."

By this time I could barely control my enthusiasm. I continued, "How would you like to see a portrait in water color of Kukolnik by his friend Brunellov?"

The Russian laid his cup on the desk and stared at me in amazement.

I reached into an upper drawer of the steel desk and drew out a leather-bound diary with a clasp on it in which I had protected the miniature for those six years. From its original wrapping of cheap, rough paper, I extracted the picture and handed it to him. He held the precious antique gently as one might a holy picture. He noted the date, 1840.

"You have here, my friend, a museum piece. Where in the world did you find it?"

I then gave the Russian its history. I conveyed him in fancy, from this alien land far across the Mediterranean and through the Dardanelles; over the Sea of Marmora to the mosques of the Golden Horn; then through the leafy Bosphorus, and on across the Black Sea. I told him of a day when our destroyer sailed from Constantinople to Odessa. It was in the summer of 1923 that our ship arrived at Odessa at a time when the Bolsheviks were terrorizing

the elite of that once great city of the Ukraine. Our ship
was not particularly welcome. They resented our guns
and torpedo tubes; but the American Relief Administra-
tion needed our assistance so we were tolerated.

Grass grew among the cobbles of the main boulevards.
All the woodwork had been torn from the windows and
the rooms of the handsome residences. The winter had
brought misery and death to the bourgeoisie, for the
"workers" had been in need of fuel.

I had been assigned the task of studying the religious
situation there. The American high commissioner at Constantinople desired an investigation of the so-called "Living Church" which attracted attention at the time. An
interpreter met me on the quay one Sunday morning, and
we started in quest of facts about sealed churches, open
churches, the why and the wherefore, and all the rest that
goes with that sort of a report on "conditions." But that
is another story. After a full morning of fact-finding, the
interpreter suggested that I meet some of his friends. . . .
I would find them interesting but desperately unhappy.

We entered the massive stone entrance of an apartment
building and climbed three flights of dingy stairway. I had
the uncomfortable certainty of being followed, and turned
and looked over the banister. I was right. There below
were two evil-looking officials in visored caps and leather
boots. My companion held me by the arm. "We're being
followed. . . . They've been following us all morning.
But don't let it worry you. They wonder what I'm up
to. Tomorrow it may be my turn in the courtyard." He
had told me about the Cheka and the daily executions in
Odessa.

We stopped at an ugly oaken door at the head of the

stairs, and the interpreter tapped what seemed to be a code message. The door was opened by a bearded old man who greeted the interpreter affectionately. He led us into a large, high-ceilinged room whose every wall was completely covered with beautiful paintings. More men, about eight in all, appeared from an adjoining room; all artists, it was apparent. They were pale, emaciated and obviously despondent. But they seemed to be pleased to see me; their eyes brightened as though new hope had climbed the stairs with us. The old man stood to one side and permitted the younger artists to take charge. Occasionally one pointed to the smaller pictures on the wall, and then they would discuss some mysterious possibility. All would then pause and stare at me appealingly, like hungry children begging food. At last the interpreter turned to me and said, "Those fellows are desperate. . . . They need money to escape with. They want you to take a valuable picture with you and sell it for them when they give the word."

Such a procedure would have placed me in a position of no little embarrassment. Carrying a canvas under my arm, in uniform, through the streets of Odessa, under the eyes of suspicious secret agents, did not square with my idea of propriety. It might cause unpleasantness at the quay, if not serious complications as well in the artists' apartment.

It was not easy to tell them this for they were sensitive men, unhappy lovers of beauty and of peaceful living. They represented to me the best that was left of Russia, and they were desperately clinging to a modicum of hope. When the old man of the white beard fell to his knees and wept, I gave in. Nor am I sorry that I relented. With money from the sale of a picture, they might possibly escape across the Rumanian frontier, perhaps through bribery.

Did they have, I inquired, a very small picture, one of sufficient value, that I might conceal beneath my blouse? In astonishment they conferred, and finally brought forth the little portrait painted and inscribed in 1840 by Brunellov.

For many years I have waited—I am still waiting— for word from Odessa. The portrait is framed now, and it is "standing by" in a distinguished place on the friendly bulkhead of my room in the U.S.S. *California*, flagship of the battle force.

CHAPTER 26

A Cheer for the Pope

AFTER Barcelona, our next port of call was Naples where a chance was given all hands to visit the old city's interesting environs—Pompeii, Vesuvius, Capri and the rest. But the thought in everyone's mind was Rome—an overnight stay in the Eternal City and an audience with the Holy Father.

There were to be two large parties, one on Saturday, the other on Monday, each made up of five hundred men. The first group left the ships early in the morning and found a special train chartered to take them on this memorable adventure. It was exciting, for most of the lads were about to have their first ride on a continental train and to order their first lunch in an Italian dining car. The chef on that run made an enviable reputation.

They told us, on our arrival at Rome, that His Holiness, Pope Pius XI, would grant an audience to our party at five that afternoon. This allowed a few hours for sight-seeing and time to buy rosary beads and medals to be blessed by the Beloved Vicar of Christ.

Promptly at the appointed hour we assembled in the audience room. The Holy Father had been strolling in the garden and he seemed the picture of health; his twenty-minute address indicated vigor and strength. He was then in his late seventies. The Rector of the North American College, my old friend, Monsignor Eugene S. Burke, translated the speech for us and then turned to me and suggested that I propose three cheers for the Holy Father. He thought this might ease the tension; all hands had maintained studious silence up to this moment.

As soon as I made the announcement, a midshipman—he who had addressed me at the movies our first night at sea—proved quick on the draw. He rose and shouted, "Let's give a 4-N yell for Pius XI." Five hundred voices in perfect unison rendered for the first time in the history of the Vatican, the Naval Academy's cheer of victory: N-N-N-N . . . A-A-A-A . . . V-V-V-V . . . Y-Y-Y-Y . . . Naaaavy . . . Pius XI."

I was much relieved on discovering the Holy Father smiling and clapping his hands. The Rector of the American College explained to the Holy Father that this was the American collegiate way of rendering high honor. The great Pope approved and he again clapped his hands.

The midshipman squadron, faithful to a long tradition, invariably seeks an audience with the Roman pontiff. The Holy Father said on that day that the officers and men of the American Navy were always particularly welcome at the Vatican.

A cheer for the Holy Father! Would we were able this year to cheer the heart of our beloved Pius XII. The midshipmen will not visit Rome this summer, but many hundreds on this year's practice cruise in the Caribbean will pray for his intention. They will pray for peace, and may God grant that their prayers be heard.

CHAPTER 27

China Bound

WHEN the officers and men left Rome to rejoin the midshipman practice squadron at Naples, I suddenly faced the happy reality of being on a leave of absence which naval officers dream about. To be in a ship at sea with full dominion over the hours—free of daily quarters for muster, drills, conferences and inspections—was a prospect that made me quite content.

Everything had worked out well. The two audiences with Pope Pius XI edified all hands; the midshipmen and sailors were pleased with the tours that I had arranged for them through Thomas Cook & Son; and finally the visit with my old school friend, Monsignor Burke. While in Rome, word came that my cousin, Mrs. Charles Tilghman, and her four children were motoring from Lourdes to join me at Marseilles for a few days before the sailing of the *d'Artagnan*. I met them there and we had a perfect holiday motoring over the French countryside and sampling, in the evening, the celebrated cuisine of the restaurants of Marseilles. They came aboard ship to bid me *bon voyage* and they stood long on the dock, waving, as the ship stood out the bay to take me halfway around the globe to a tour of duty in the destroyer squadron of the Asiatic Fleet.

The *d'Artagnan* of the Messageries Maritimes was a

handsome ship of about 20,000 tons. Most of her passengers were French army officers and their families, bound for Indo-China. The senior among them was a slender, dapper general who paced the deck with the verve and vigor of an Irish terrier. He and his military shipmates and their wives invariably came to breakfast dressed in silk pajamas, and they remained thus attired until shortly before luncheon when they changed to sports clothes. For dinner, the officers dressed formally in their uniforms. It was amusing the way they shook hands each morning when they met on deck. It was a racial custom that the lone Englishman, Smythe, vehemently disliked. Smythe was a short, swarthy fellow in the employ of the Asiatic Petroleum Company. He dreaded the prospect of returning to Manila where he had already given ten years of service. Completely fed up with the Orient, he found it a bore that I should respond to the fascinating allure of the East.

Although I enjoyed the company of my cosmopolitan shipmates, I rather suspected those travelling second class were in many ways more lively and interesting. When the first entertainment was held in the salon, we discovered that second cabin boasted a Viennese orchestra, booked for an engagement at Surabaya, Java. They injected a spirit of frivolity whenever they appeared publicly but especially during the hot nights before the monsoon gave some relief to our discomfort in the Indian Ocean, and earlier when we steamed through the Red Sea. One of the performers at a musicale was a Chinese boy prodigy who had mastered the violin in Paris. He played with high distinction.

I found this collection of varied types among the passengers of ever-increasing interest. Seeing them every day, playing deck games and chatting with them on promenades, made it easy to learn what they had done and how they had planned for the future. There was a young Siamese army officer who had spent four years under instruction with the British Army. He spun many yarns about life in the various regiments, all of which he had enjoyed.

One evening after dinner, when the ship was in the Indian Ocean, a group sat at a round table on topside telling stories. The general, a few majors, the Siamese, a French schoolteacher, a Chinese named Mr. Li, Smythe, the Englishman, and myself formed a strange mélange of personalities. When the general asked the French civilian whether he had fought in the World War and, if so, what rank he had achieved before the end, the teacher, with unconcealed gusto replied, "*Mon General*, I entered the war a buck private and I came out a buck private." We clapped our hands in approval. Mr. Li, the Chinese, in polished French, congratulated the modest schoolteacher and thanked him for this chance to meet the only man he had ever seen who was willing to admit that he had not attained in the war to at least the exalted rank of lieutenant. It reminded me that Joyce Kilmer chose to remain a sergeant in the A.E.F.

Later that evening I asked the Chinese linguist where he had acquired his command of French. The others at table heard me and they too were interested when Li replied he had studied four years at the University of Louvain, graduating as an engineer in 1911. That was the year I had entered. We promptly celebrated in the traditional way this reunion of two Louvain alumni.

At Colombo, an Englishman, named Ashley, joined us for the passage to Singapore. His ultimate destination was Java where he planned to study the rubber situation. He told of experiences he had recently had in Africa where he had trekked in a safari into Liberia. One day, when he appointed a new foreman of the safari, he learned a lesson in human nature. He chose from the gang of natives a huge black and gave him his orders. The foreman had but one request—that he be given a rifle to carry, a symbol of authority. Thereupon he started down the trail and struck each black over the head with the butt of the gun. There was no question from then on who was boss.

Ashley told of a weird incident on a lion hunt in Africa. One evening he and his fellow-hunters came upon a lion. They stood to leeward which made their presence unknown to the beast. The lion stood beneath a tree whose top branches were filled with squealing monkeys. He assumed a rigid stance, with his head lifted, and he gazed fixedly upon the frightened monkeys until one fell, landing so close to the lion that he crushed it with a quick slap of his paw. With his jaws, he caught the dead monkey by the tail and swung it over his back and then continued to gaze aloft, hypnotizing his next victim. When the jungle king had six monkeys thus acquired for his evening meal, he turned to leave. But Ashley, with his trusty gun, laid him low.

Ashley talked far into the night. He knew his Africa.

The *d'Artagnan* remained ten days at Saigon. The heat was oppressive. I welcomed the chance to go on a trip to Pnom Pehn in Cambodia. We motored the three hundred kilometers in a big Fiat, through immense rice paddies and crossed the wide Mekong on a barge. Pnom Pehn came nearest to my preconceived notions regarding an oriental city. Buddhist priests in their saffron-colored gowns walked the streets like mendicant friars seeking alms. I took movies of the sacred white elephants of the king and I found it weird to see the cobra motif in sculptured decorations on the many bridges I crossed in my ramblings through town.

The French passengers left us at Saigon, and Smythe at Hong Kong. Mr. Li and his wife, a bit weary of French cooking, went ashore there for a dinner of Chinese food but they were unable to find anyone who spoke their northern dialect. Li said he thought it ridiculous to be forced to speak English in his native land. They had tiffin with us in a hotel near the landing.

At Shanghai, I reported my arrival to the senior American naval officer present, Commander James M. Doyle, skipper of a gunboat to the Yangtze patrol. He delivered my orders that afternoon in the Shanghai Club on the Bund. An old friend of the Turkish Station, Dr. Wendell Perry, came with us. That evening at the Hotel Majestic, I enjoyed a delightful dinner party with the Perrys.

On a Sunday afternoon, I had my luggage taken to the Bund where I boarded a little coastal steamer for Chefoo. My companion on that interesting voyage was Lieutenant Kendall Reed who had orders to my old ship, the *McCormick*.

I reported for duty on board the tender *Black Hawk* looking forward hopefully to a two-year cruise in the Far East.

CHAPTER 28

The "Asiatics"

THE sailors of the squadron spoke of the Far East as the "Asiatics." Officers normally called it the "China Station." The enlisted men evidently had in mind the expansive area comprising the Netherland East Indies, Singapore, the Celebes, the Philippines and Japan—wherever the annual tours of goodwill might take them.

The two years I spent in the Asiatic Fleet passed quickly because we were continually on the move. The fall I arrived on the China Station, I made a cruise to the southern islands of the Philippines in my former sea home of the eastern Mediterranean—the destroyer *McCormick*. Her commanding officer was Lieutenant Commander Francis C. Denebrink; the executive officer, Lieutenant Kendall S. Reed. The able and popular Denebrink, knowing of my fondness for the *"Micky"* and her crew, invited me to go along. He also included my shipmate and shoregoing companion, Lieutenant Commander George Barry Wilson, who was then chief of staff for the squadron commander, Captain John G. Church.

Barry and I boarded the *McCormick* at the Cavite Navy Yard. They assigned me a bunk in the same starboard room forward that I had occupied years before on cruises in the Black Sea. Several of my old sailor friends were still aboard holding their own in positions that had grown in importance with their progress in wisdom and sea experience. The ship was the same proud *"Micky,"* smart and clean. The old timers saw to that; and her skipper was one of the best.

Visiting the islands of the Philippine Archipelago was one of the "side-shows" of the Asiatic cruise. The peaceful little ports of Luzon, Panay, Negros and Mindanao knew the American sailor and they showed in many ways they were glad to see him come. The day the *McCormick* stood in at Doumeguette we spied a Filipino boy scout standing on the top of a tall column which served as a lighthouse. As we approached the anchorage in the late afternoon, our signalman caught the semaphore message, "Welcome to our port." Captain Denebrink replied: "Son, send this message and slowly. 'We are glad to be here.'"

The next day the local baseball team gave the *McCormick's* "varsity" a good trimming before a large crowd of excited fans.

The *McCormick* was the flagship of Commander Stewart Brown, Commander of the Thirty-ninth Division. He usually asked me to accompany him on his official visits to provincial governors. The first call was impressive. From the moment we left the dock to our arrival at the governor's office, everything was done with punctilio. The little capitol which stood in the center of a large park fringed with coco palms boasted a façade of four Grecian columns. We found the provincial governor in an office on the second floor, flanked by a dozen or more of his official family. The governor spoke no English but he had a young interpreter who quickly translated into Spanish. Most of the governors we met spoke English fluently,

especially the one we called on in Zamboanga, a graduate
of the University of Michigan. It seemed to me the main
purpose of those visits was to arrange for a party either at
the governor's palace or on board the *McCormick*. They
were always wholesome fun.

One afternoon, during our stay in Iloilo, a group of
McCormick officers—Stewart, Denebrink, Wilson, Nick-
erson and myself—called on the local Ordinary, Bishop
McClosky. We spent a pleasant hour with the distinguished prelate, a former Philadelphian, and enjoyed his
hospitality. The following day His Excellency was our
guest at luncheon on the fo'c'sle of the *McCormick*.

At Iloilo I was introduced to the "lizard game" which,
they said, an old army colonel had invented to facilitate
determining who was to sign the chit when playmates
assembled on the porch of the club. One evening our
American friends took us to the club. It was a moonlit
night, cool and exotic. I recall the little lights flickering on
the waters of the bay and playful lizards scampering across
the wall near which we were sitting. There were fifteen
of us at a huge, round mahogany table. As the evening
progressed, one of the *McCormick* officers asked if he
might buy a round of drinks. It was then proposed that we
play the lizard game.

A barefoot Filipino in a long white gown was told to
catch a lizard. While he was reaching up the side of the
wall in pursuit of one, another servant placed a leather
dice-box in the center of the table and two dice in front
of each person to serve as markers for a sort of alleyway.
When the lizard was caught, the boy dropped it into the
dice-box and made it prisoner by laying a flat ash tray on
top of the box. At a given signal, the ash tray was removed

and the lizard slowly emerged. Its little dragonlike head wove back and forth and then, like a flash of light, it made for one of the alleys, coming to a dead stop on someone's chest. The person thus favored by the lizard signed the chit. We learned later that a dark necktie (which the local men seldom wore) held an especial attraction for the lizard. Its vision being affected by the darkness in the dice-box this looked to it like a sure way of escape. Strangers usually lost in the last accounting, but occasionally a recalcitrant lizard upset the old timers' predictions, and this kept all hands, especially the women, in gleeful suspense.

One day at the Manila Army and Navy Club I met John Ford, the distinguished director of motion pictures. He had taken a long sea jaunt with George O'Brien, the movie star, whom I had met years before in New York when he was making the picture, "East Side, West Side." The following day they were my guests for lunch on the lawn of the Polo Club. I hurriedly gathered some of the young destroyer skippers to meet them, among whom were Commander "Pop" Gillam, Lieutenant Commanders "Possum" Webb and the late Valentine Wood. I believe Barry Wilson also was there. It was a grand party with the brilliant John Ford "carrying the ball."

I have since met John Ford several times in Hollywood. I shall always remember the day he invited my sister Anita and me to lunch in the commissary of the Twentieth Century Fox Studio. We met many celebrities of the screen that day.

What chiefly struck me on a tour of the studios was the extraordinary and painstaking hard labor the director and the actors showed in working out a simple paragraph or two of the script. What with the countless rehearsals of lines and business, it often took an hour to attain the desired artistic effect.

Before Commander Barry Wilson, his wife Anne, and their four children embarked for "homeside," I baptized their baby, Ruth, who had recently appeared on the Asiatic scene in Shanghai. The Baptism was held in the Cathedral in the old walled city of Manila.

In the summer of 1930, the Chefoo Club was the hub of the social whirl for the navy people. The terrace ran from the building to the sea-wall and it served both the British and Americans as a pleasant gathering place for cocktails and formal dinner parties.

My room at the club was on the second floor. Beyond the French windows was a porch large enough for a table, accommodating ten people for dinner. The Chinese "boy," Chin, then in his early fifties, was exemplary in every way. He was so well trained to care for the needs of the "European" that at first I found his thoroughness running counter to my ideas of democracy. Returning from the tennis courts my first day at the club, I found that Chin had already laid out on the bed a complete change of clothing, along with a walking stick and a box of matches. When I returned from the bath, which I took in a big, round, earthen jar that another boy had filled with hot water carried up from the basement, Chin knelt down beside me to lace my shoes. The British had trained him, but I immediately strove to lighten his burdens without intending to lessen his willingness to serve. Chin was a marvel. All I had to say was, "Chin, tonight eight piecie for dinner." He replied, "Can do, Master." When I returned from the terrace with my friends, we found a beautifully appointed table, flowers and candles, and Chin, in immaculate white gown, taking charge as I had never seen it done before. Chin might have graced the pages of Somerset Maugham's "On a Chinese Screen."

"Dolly" Fitzgerald and I, after he came north from the Yangtze patrol where he had served as flag lieutenant for Rear Admiral T. T. Craven, made our liberties together. Occasionally after tennis we dropped in at the original, "Cloob 49," which was commissioned that summer in Room 49 of the Grand Hotel. The charter members were, among a few others whose names I have forgotten, Denebrink, Pickhardt, McDowell and "Pay" Carroll. Following tennis at the courts across the road, they invited their friends to cold beer and cheese. It was a Chefoo counterpart of a Paris salon where one met only the most congenial members of the colony.

The next summer, Lieutenant Commander Adolf Pickhardt, who later became our naval attaché in Berlin, sent me a dispatch from the Yangtze asking me to revive "Cloob 49" and to choose a new place because the landlord at the Grand Hotel had raised the rent. With "Fitz" and the late "Baron" Long, I set out to find a suitable Cloob house. At the Beach Café, we learned that Ross, the owner, had a vacant house a five-minute rickshaw ride from the courts. We took it, and had a piano installed. To our surprise, after the servants had polished the front gate, the number on the wall was 49. A happy coincidence. I sent a dispatch to "Pick" that all was in readiness for a season at the modernized Cloob. The house was built of stone; we entertained in the living room. Only beer and cheese were served in this simple rendezvous of tennis enthusiasts. On one of the walls, a yeoman from the *Black Hawk* painted a tennis player in shorts. In one hand the gay fellow held aloft a racquet; in the other, a stein of beer. Surrounding him were written the toasts of many lands—"Salud"; "Here's How"; "Cheerio"; "Banzai"; "Skoll"; "Schlante" and "Mud in your Eye!" On another wall was a huge chart on which "Fitz" kept the beer score. The Cloob's version of the Heidelberg salamander was "Einz, zwei, drei—Mug Up!"

One always found gayety and song in "Cloob 49." Our membership grew steadily with the arrival of new bachelors to the squadron. Commander M. C. Robertson, who is now the chief of staff of the scouting force, was the senior member that summer.

"Cloob 49" could always be counted on to take part in the Saturday night masquerades at the Chefoo Club. Our masterpiece in the summer of 1931 was a bull fight. We had our Chinese tailors make appropriate costumes and a magnificent bull. Tom Marshall was the bow and "Dolly" Fitzgerald was the stern. Little Nancy Hurt was the queen of the bull fight and she rode the bull's back in the splendiferous parade which preceded the burlesque of our Castilian *carrida*.

We spent the winter months in Manila. The wives and children came south, following the ships, and set up housekeeping again in attractive apartments in the modern sections of the city. As spring approached with its depressing heat, many went to the army camp at Baguio, high in the mountains of Luzon. We slept there under two or three blankets. It reminded me of the Poconos.

CHAPTER 29

The Good Shepherd of Chefoo

IN THE spring, about the time the Manila sun became oppressive, the destroyer squadron of the Asiatic Fleet customarily weighed anchor and set a course for Hong Kong. In all, there were eighteen destroyers in our force, and the *Black Hawk* was the mother ship; she was a veritable floating navy yard, and managed to keep her lively brood in good repair.

After a week in Hong Kong, where many happy excursions were made, we headed north for a longer stay at Amoy. There the squadron commander held the annual military inspections of the ships. But there was ample time for shopping tours in the old town and for long hikes over the hills. The popular purchase there was the Amoy cat—a realistic little toy of papier-mâché whose head nodded at the gentlest urging.

Next on the schedule came Shanghai, that marvelous city of weird contradictions. Here West met East but they never quite became acquainted. Shanghai was a gay place ten years ago, and a great favorite with the men. We enjoyed life along the Bund: the indefatigable coolies, chanting as they lugged their heavy burdens; the little coastal steamers moored at the quay; the hundreds of sampans and clumsy junks and the great ocean liners and warships at anchor in the Whangpoo.

The spring cruise which ended at Chefoo in North China was leisurely. It was a sort of breathing spell that came between seasons of gunnery practice. We were again in blue uniforms, and we welcomed the exhilarating crisp air of the North.

We spent a week at Tsingtao and then steamed up the coast to Chinwang Tao. This was the jumping off place for a train ride to Peking. All hands were granted several days leave of absence in the ancient capital, where they saw beautiful traces of the imperial glory of old Cathay.

The squadron arrived at Chefoo in the last week of May, and the ships based there until late in the fall.

When I had first reported for duty in September, 1929, Chefoo was just recovering from the shock of a local war. A new war lord—a military gangster named General Lu —had won a decisive battle to the southward of the town; and the aftermath of his conquest was still in evidence. I learned about it one day when our ship's doctor took me with him on a visitation of the Catholic hospital. There I found the French nuns caring for thirty-five or more Chinese soldiers. Their ears had been cut off; their backs had been beaten with split bamboo rods which had torn the flesh to ribbons. Also they were mortally ill with dysentery. The hospital had no physician but our navy surgeon, Dr. William D. Davis, volunteered his services. Several navy wives charitably assisted the nuns in nursing the wounded.

As far as I was concerned, the chief citizen of Chefoo was the beloved bishop, a Frenchman and a member of the Franciscan Order. He did not look his age, nor had the vicissitudes of life under the yoke of a Chinese war lord lessened his optimism and missionary zeal. He was of medium height, and he wore a light gray silk soutane. His Van Dyke beard, which was always carefully trimmed, helped to give the impression that he might be an animated, medieval churchman, lately removed from a museum painting. He was hospitable and easy to talk to. I can still see him after the navy Mass on Sunday mornings standing in the center of a group of children and their parents, chatting in the courtyard of his cathedral. He was especially fond of our squadron commander, a non-Catholic whose wife and children attended the nine o'clock Mass. It must have pleased him to learn that Captain Isaac F. Dortch was the one who secretly paid for the screens which were placed in the windows of the children's orphanage; and his soul must have rejoiced to learn that his good friend the captain became a Catholic shortly before he died.

The bishop lived in a large mission house adjacent to the small but solidly built cathedral. On occasion he invited me to lunch with him. I recall how expert he was with chopsticks. He could actually, with those chopsticks, pick up from his plate a single little French pea. It was a clever stunt that had all the intriguing humor of a parlor trick. He gave me my first lesson in the use of that strange twin device of the Chinese dinner table; but I proved woefully inadequate, and I had eventually to plead for a fork.

The bishop took me on a tour of the mission establishments. He showed me first the stately little cathedral, built of gray stone. Its history interested me, for I celebrated Mass there for my navy people during our stay at Chefoo. Like almost everything else one saw in China there was here too an element of surprise. The cathedral was the gift of a Scotsman. As I recall the bishop's story, the good man, many years previously, had lost his fortune when a typhoon had destroyed his fleet of sea-going junks.

But, undismayed, he called on the bishop one day and promised that, should he ever again become prosperous, he would build a cathedral. The bishop showed a plaque on the wall which bears witness to the merchant's fidelity. The edifice stands as an abiding monument to the Scotsman's gratitude.

Not far from the cathedral is the orphanage where I was shown several girl babies who might have been done away with but for the nuns. Unfeeling fathers often demand that they be removed from the home, pleading poverty as their motive. The nuns take them in and train them to sew and to do many useful things. I still have sets of vestments which the little Chefoo girls embroidered; they are works of art. During my first summer at Chefoo the children of the orphanage made a complete set of summer vestments for Pope Pius XI; they were as light as a feather.

The bishop was justly proud of his *oeuvres*, as he called the many activities he had instituted and administered at Chefoo. He was worried, however, for fear the latest war lord might interfere with the running of his school. It was in the able hands of the Christian Brothers, but General Lu had been sending his agents to inspect, and their attitude was not friendly.

One morning the bishop and I started out to visit the orphanage and the school. I was hungry for knowledge about the progress of our missionaries in China. I addressed the bishop: "Your Excellency, what about the Church's progress in China? Do you ever become discouraged?"

He replied: "At this moment I am heart-sick from worry. The bandits in the hills are holding two of my priests for ransom, but I believe they'll be returned unharmed. One is never free of problems in this country. There is great poverty, and poverty leads to crime. As for conversions; well, when I came here forty-five years ago, I knew I shouldn't be able to convert China. I was determined though to do all in my power to win souls to Christ. We have made some progress."

We were nearing the Bund at the seaside where the street swings back into town again. Just as we turned the corner, three well-dressed Chinese women cut across the street at a sharp angle and greeted the bishop in their native language. Each kissed the prelate's ring and carried on an animated conversation. There was laughter and confusion for they all seemed to be talking in chorus. It was a picture symbolic of the good shepherd.

The bishop explained later that the three Chinese women had once been undesired girl babies, left at the doorstep of the orphanage. The nuns had cared for them for many years, educated them and fitted them for an independent place in the community. Now they were married to wealthy merchants of Chefoo. It was obvious that they were happy. Two of the husbands had already embraced the Faith; their children were in the convent school.

This simple episode cheered the good bishop's heart. "You see," he said, "to convert China requires years, maybe centuries of patient labor. It is a slow process."

I learned a little while ago that the good shepherd of Chefoo is no longer on the quest for souls. He has been called to report in Heaven to his Maker of his stewardship in the province of Shantung.

CHAPTER 30

Tolerance in China

LOOKING through my papers the other day I ran across a piece I wrote ten years ago for *The Commonweal*. It illustrates the unusual position a Catholic navy chaplain may be required to assume in the far corners of the earth. It is called "Tolerance in China."

"The first step upon the Chefoo jetty may jar one's American sensibilities, but there is unmistakably a composite gesture of welcome everywhere. The mob of rickshaw coolies, most of them smarting under the batons of local constables, mill about you like a sort of greeters' committee shouting, 'Me take, master, me take.' Their celebrated rickshaws garnished with tin and lace invite you and if you succeed in climbing aboard without tripping over a canine 'wonk,' you may count on a pleasant though jerky promenade down the Bund.

"Chefoo lies on the northern shore of the Shantung peninsula, about eighty miles to the southward across the Lao-tie-shan Channel from Port Arthur. This territory is ruled capably by the iron fist of a swashbuckling war-lord named Liu. He has more notches on his gun than Jesse James ever dreamed of. Liu boasts of 35,000 well-drilled hirelings and defies the whole of celestial Cathay, regardless of the threats of Chiang Kai Chek, Chang Hsueh-Liang and the rest. The general rather fancies basketball;

you will find him often at the Y compound cheering his officers to victory over the destroyer sailors.

"Missionaries are solidly established there, and the town serves too as a pleasant resort for Europeans seeking cool relief from the heat of summer. The Asiatic Fleet has held rendezvous at Chefoo for many years. But the problem of providing suitable recreation for the enlisted men has always been a source of worry to their elders. This problem was partly solved when the Y.M.C.A. built their recreation center near the jetty. It is a marvelous place, this navy Y with its soda-fountain, restaurant, library, boxing-room, tennis courts and auditorium. It is mainly with the auditorium that this story deals, because it was there that I discovered a high quality of religious tolerance worthy perhaps of the telling.

"At ten-thirty of a Sunday morning the navy Y is a busy place. The huge banner which is slung across the street catches the eye as one comes up from the landing. It carries the legend, 'Fleet Church.' And a good advertisement it is, for it attracts to the auditorium many officers and their children, bluejackets, American missionaries and representatives of the British colony.

"The concert by the sailors' band is over and the choir, composed of sailors and missionary children, are poised for the opening hymn. The pianist, whose three children are members of the choir, is the wife of the superintendent of the Presbyterian hospital on Temple Hill. A young Y secretary directs the singing. Standing on a dais beneath a large white cross I begin with prayer. I had just rickshawed over from the cathedral, where a little while before I had celebrated Holy Mass. That morning I had chatted in the cathedral garden with the saintly old bishop, long removed from his beloved France, who said: 'Ah, *monsieur l'aumonier*, again you become a lighthouse for the other people.'

" 'Thank you, Bishop,' was the reply. 'I hope I shan't be a dim one.'

" 'Tell me, my son,' inquired the bishop, 'how did it come about that you were given this interesting assignment?'

"I told the venerable missionary of a spring evening in 1930 when the chaplains of the Asiatic Fleet held a *gaudeamus* at the Manila Polo Club.

" 'We're all great buddies, Monseigneur, and we welcome a chance to fan the breeze (if you get what I mean) over our experiences. And there's probably no lovelier place in all the world to spend an evening than on the festive lawn of the polo club. We had the dinner placed beneath oriental lanterns near the sea-wall, within earshot of the waves that wash the shores of Manila Bay. The chairs were set widely enough apart to permit the Filipino boys to "flit" the air at brief intervals. It was funny the way they came every five minutes and pumped the gun under the table. But the voracious mosquitoes of Luzon were also in conference that evening. A memorable occasion, I assure you. . . . Not far in the darkness that hovered over the bay, the man-of-war lights glimmered where the destroyer swung peacefully at anchor. There was charm in the moonlight on that tropic lawn, whose serenity was calculated to warm the cockles of any human heart, let alone those gold-braid servants of the Nazarene who, though divided in their respective loyalties and disciplines, were, nonetheless, united in friendship and in their desire to serve God and souls.

" 'The destroyer squadron whose summer base was at Chefoo had acquired me, a Catholic priest, as chaplain. What would become of the non-denominational service known as *"Fleet Church"*? That was the chief topic of discussion.

" 'At the table was a group of Protestant ministers, a Baptist, an Episcopalian, two Methodists, and myself. In a few days the Fleet would head for northern waters, and the navy families, too, like birds of passage would follow after, to build in North China their temporary nests, in circumstances trying both to body and soul. The ministers demanded then that I assume charge of the Protestant parish.'

" 'Ah!' the good bishop interrupted with a smile. 'They must have enjoyed the Burgundy.'

" 'Well,' I continued, 'this proposal, in spite of many years of happy association with Protestant chaplains of the Navy, rather shocked at first. Following closely as it did upon the recent campaign of ill feeling among the voters of the United States, their decision acquired an especial importance. But would Chefoo stand for it? Would the Protestants come to hear the sermons of a priest? The ministers persisted. "They'll come. . . . Don't worry . . . and the best of luck." '

" 'Yours is a grand opportunity, my son,' the old prelate said. 'I wish you success.'

"He had labored among the Chinese for forty-five long years. In the garden of St. Mary's that day in June the bishop approved of Fleet Church, and with great feeling he commended a congregation of exiles who were welcoming a 'lighthouse' for, said he, 'Are they not seeking the kindly light of truth?'

"Chefoo, that summer and the summer following, experienced the unusual. Protestants of various denominations listened week in and week out to Catholic sermons on the Gospel of the day. They listened to the same words that were spoken each Sunday from the altar of St. Mary's.

"The experience was a trying one but I believe, for me, it was highly beneficial. Never have I worked so hard on my sermons. It was encouraging to have the congregation come to me after the services and say, 'I so enjoyed your message.' "

CHAPTER 31

Boxing in Bangkok

ONE evening some time later at the Manila Polo Club I received a bit of good news. The late Captain Halsey Powell, who commanded the old armored cruiser, *Pittsburgh*, asked me whether I would like to join his ship on a de luxe cruise to Siam and the Netherlands East Indies. The *Pittsburgh* as flagship of the Asiatic Fleet had been relieved by the new heavy cruiser, *Houston*, and was now to set forth on her last of a long series of voyages to carry Americans of high rank to friendly peoples of the seven seas. The Governor General of the Philippines, Dwight F. Davis, was to take the *Pittsburgh* on a six-weeks' tour of good will. The itinerary called for visits to the Governor of Indo-China, the King of Siam, the British of the Malay States and the Dutch of Sumatra, Java, Bali and Makassar.

Without the slightest hesitancy and with ardent enthusiasm, I accepted the captain's invitation. I was delighted to know that my old shipmate, Lieutenant Commander Francis C. Denebrink, was to be the governor's naval aide. The military aide was Lieutenant Colonel Maxwell Murray, U.S.A. He is now a major general in command of Schofield Barracks on the island of Oahu. The ship's executive officer was Commander Preston B. Haines who now commands the cruiser, *Astoria*. In the governor general's party, in addition to the members of his cabinet, were Cynthia Davis and Dwight, Junior.

The *Pittsburgh* sailed from Manila in the middle of April, 1931. All hands, even the coal heavers of the black gang, were in high spirits over this extraordinary chance to visit the most interesting ports of the Far East.

Our distinguished shipmate soon gave us many reasons to be proud of him. At the Tennis Club of Saigon the donor of the Davis Cup and his son defeated the best doubles team of Indo-China. That evening we attended a state dinner in the palace of the French governor. Not only was the exterior of the palace completely illuminated with electric lights but the large bamboo trees on the landscaped lawn also glistened in colored brilliance. The *Pittsburgh*, moored at the river quay, was also rigged with thousands of lights, outlining her contour for the admiration of the natives who came in droves to admire the old flagship. At the dinner with over a hundred guests, Mr. Davis, wearing a miniature of his Distinguished Service Cross, replied to the governor's speech of welcome in impeccable French.

During the passage from Saigon across the Gulf of Siam, I rounded up the boxers and staged a smoker. The *Pittsburgh* carried several of the Fleet's best fighters. They had been ordered to her for passage to the United States. This joy ride of the old flagship was but a prelude to the homeward bound cruise to the States via the Suez Canal. While sitting at the ringside that night, I recalled what I had read of boxing in Siam and I wondered whether the entertainment committee of Bangkok had included boxing in the agenda. The thought of it rather weakened my ardor for the bluejacket type of mutual massacre, for Siamese fighting had been represented as having the elements of jungle ferocity. I made up my mind to see the boxing in Bangkok. I was interested in view of my many years' experience as a promoter of the sport in the Navy.

The ship anchored at the mouth of the river Medan, for the chart showed a sand bar in our path which served as a natural barrier against the intrusion of ships of war. That afternoon the captain suggested that I go with him to Bangkok and make plans for the entertainment of the crew. Parties of two hundred would make the trip each way by train. When a messenger reported to me that the gig was alongside, my Filipino mess boy was still packing my things. I told him to bear a hand. In his hurry, he failed to secure the fastenings of the bag, a fact I learned to my amazement a few minutes later. The captain was already in the boat when I arrived at the gangway. There was quite a sea running and the gig was tossing dizzily. Needing both hands, I threw in the suitcase and made a jump for it. Alas, when I was safe aboard, I found my linens, toilet articles and shoes strewn over the deck. The captain laughed but my face was red.

The gig took us to a Siamese gunboat that lay a thousand yards from our anchorage. Word had come that the ebbing tide made it imperative that we cross the sand bar at once. As soon as we climbed aboard, the Siamese skipper ordered "full speed ahead" and bounced the little war craft over the bar as one would drive a truck over a plowed field.

Strange-looking automobiles passed slowly along the main street of Bangkok. They were of such an early vintage I might have thought they were advertisements of a rummage sale if they had not been painted a shiny royal yellow and driven by chauffeurs in livery. The cars chugged along at the approved speed of 1904. These earliest of American models had been reposing in the king's garages for many years like postage stamps in an album. The late king was a collector of cars. When he died they distributed his collection among his royal though poor relations. All that was needed to complete a gay nineties tableau was a Gibson girl in a linen duster and a picture hat tied down by a flowing veil.

Our minister to Siam, David E. Kaufman, I quickly discovered, was a devotee of boxing. When we first met at the legation, he asked me to help him work out a scheme he had been developing since he first heard that an American man o' war was to visit Siam. Would it be possible, he inquired, to obtain a half dozen sailor-boxers from the *Pittsburgh* to stage exhibition bouts that week at the Suan S'nuk Arena? He deplored the brutality of the Siamese version of the sport; participants were often severely if not fatally hurt. Mr. Kaufman had already succeeded in getting the local promoters to adopt the American glove in lieu of the thick cord the boxers used for binding their knuckles. Formerly, he said, a hard blow to the body caused the flesh to be cut as though with a buzz saw. There were to be the usual professional bouts at Suan S'nuk the following Friday. Three bouts in the American manner following the regular card would be all that was needed to convince the local fight fans that the art of "modified murder" need not be taken quite so seriously by the Siamese.

I sent a dispatch to the ship inviting six of our best battlers to come to Bangkok as guests of the Suan S'nuk. When they came, I warned them that medals and cups had been bought for them and that they would have to "put out plenty" to rate winning them. I could tell they little knew what they were up against. All they seemed to gather from what I told them was that their bouts were to be the main attraction of a fight night in Bangkok for the amusement of natives who had not as yet witnessed "the real thing."

Our sailors arrived at the arena and changed to their fighting togs. In their fancy navy blue-and-gold bath robes, they strutted importantly down the aisle, acknowledging the cheers of the excited throng with clasped hands held above their heads; and they proudly took their places in a row of ringside seats.

Entering the Suan S'nuk Arena I noticed a section near the ring reserved for a miniature field hospital. I thought it might be an exhibit staged by visiting boy scouts.

When I joined the sailors in the front row reserved for this "mission for softer pugilism," a sailor pointed to a stretcher that lay on the side of the ring. "What's the idea?" he asked. "Do these guys fight with a meat axe?" Then the American minister came, accompanied by the local Tex Rickard, carrying cups and medals which he held up for the admiration of the Fleet champions.

The ring was of the usual size and it stood in the center of a large outdoor park. There was a top over it. The only unorthodox prop was the stretcher.

Amid lusty cheers of the crowd, two fighters and a referee climbed through the ropes. The boxers were glistening bronze welterweights. They were barefoot and wore a large triangular pad suspended from their belts. After they were introduced to the lively audience, an orchestra of strings and reeds played the most exotic melody I have ever heard. It had the primitive appeal of a negro spiritual. This was a signal for the fighters to fall to their knees and salaam in prayer. They remained there in profound meditation for a few minutes and then arose slowly, their faces lined with evidence of intense emotion and in slow pantomime they delivered imaginary blows of all sorts they had previously planned in their secret communion with their gods. In doing so, they caught the weird tempo and message of the music and fired themselves into a frenzy. The quiet that fell over the stadium when the orchestra stopped playing and the fighters ceased their slow, deliberate movements chilled my spine. I glanced at the American boxers and found that they were similarly affected. The gong sounded and the men squared off in the conventional pose of the pugilist. The fighters weighed about one hundred and fifty pounds and they were magnificently set up.

Only a metropolitan sports writer could do justice to what we saw that night. The fight was on. There was no sparring or stalking. Action began with one of the men leading with his knee against the other fighter's pad; then he crossed with his left to the jaw, pulled away and kicked, landing his heel on the point of his foe's chin and dropping him like a felled ox. He then fell upon his victim and delivered "rabbit punches" with his elbow. The crowd roared approval. We navy men sat there shocked and bewildered. Could a fight between men be more savage than this? The referee finally parted the men and helped the wounded boxer to his feet. The man was still able to protect himself by ducking and sidestepping until the sound of the gong ended the round.

I was amazed to learn that no blow was barred, that you

could hit a man when he was down with impunity. What little the referee did was arbitrary. Aside from avoiding being hit by wild, unavailing blows, his main function was to pass the word at the end of each bout to the stretcher-bearer. Each of the six bouts was equally ferocious. At the end the loser was thoroughly beaten into unconsciousness. The Bangkok boxers were well trained and in fine shape. This was evident after a round or two of the fastest action I have ever seen in the prize ring. They displayed extraordinary skill and stamina and I felt sorry for them. I recall one fellow who kept the Suan S'nuk customers on their feet, yelling themselves hoarse. He was flashy, in the Madison Square manner, delivering clean wallops and flooring his man in the conventional American way. He seldom led with his knee and not once did he strike his foe when down. But he evidently forgot momentarily that Siamese boxing comprises all known techniques including the French *savatte*, for in the closing round of the bout the other man, with the speed of a king cobra, stepped back and kicked him on the jaw. So much for that. The attendants carried him off unconscious and laid him gently on a cot in the sick-bay.

I turned to Mr. Kaufman and simply shook my head, agreeing with everything he said about the ferocity of Siamese fisticuffs.

But the main event was still to be staged. Again I told the sailors they must "bear down." Although they gave something far better than the usual "exhibition," throwing punches as though they meant it, the crowd thought it was a burlesque, a mere caricature of pugilism. They laughed as though our champions were clowning. It was a bit humiliating. Our men were annoyed and they tried all the harder, so much so that I feared they would never again be on speaking terms. The crowd laughed the louder. The American minister bowed his head in utter discouragement, for his experiment had failed. We of the *Pittsburgh* had seen ring fighting in Siam that would have cheered the cold heart of a Nero.

CHAPTER 32

Making a Book

W<small>HEN</small> the Governor General of the Philippines visited the East Indies in the cruiser, *Pittsburgh*, the itinerary was so attractive we decided to publish an illustrated book as a souvenir of the voyage. Being on temporary duty, I realized that the book must be ready for distribution before I rejoined the destroyer squadron on our return to Manila. The *Black Hawk* was scheduled to sail for Hong Kong that very day. The material to be gathered was so unusual and attractive that I decided it was worth a try. It was apparent that the governor's party would appreciate such a souvenir, and I was certain that the crew of the *Pittsburgh*, who were soon to return to the United States, would treasure such a permanent record of the cruise.

On the passage from Manila to Saigon, Indo-China, I sent a radio dispatch to Chaplain George S. Rentz at the Navy Yard, Cavite, asking him to be associate editor. He replied with a cheering "affirmative" and I went to work. We offered a prize for the most suitable name for the book. The winner of the prize of twenty-five pesos hit upon the title "Cruisin' Around with the Governor General." The rather lengthy title looked good, however, on the cover which Fitch, the sailor-artist, painted for us. He portrayed in color the cruiser in a blue sea under clouds that formed a map of the voyage. With small dots he traced our progress. A marine photographer, who had been sent from the Bureau to make official pictures of the governor's diplomatic visits, promised to give me a copy of all his important shots. Lieutenant Commander Denebrink, the naval aide, was to supply me with copies of press dispatches and speeches delivered by the governor general.

At Saigon we started gathering copy. The local papers featured the donor of the Davis Cup, playing tennis. I had photostats made. The marine took pictures of the illumination of the French governor's palace, and the *Pittsburgh*, draped from bow to stern with lights. But the visit to Bangkok gave promise of even greater interest. The pictures were fine; and the speeches made by the King of Siam and the governor at the state dinner made splendid copy.

It was my good fortune to be one of the guests of King Pradjahipok the night he honored our distinguished shipmate. Hundreds of Siamese nobles had already gathered in the great marble halls when we arrived. At dinner we sat at a long table, the length of a battleship, and the general setting was rich in oriental splendor. During the dinner, which was served on gold plate, an orchestra of one hundred Siamese musicians played selections from the works of Gilbert and Sullivan. I was told that only the director, who had studied music in Paris, had ever been beyond the frontiers of his native land. They played in a hidden nook of the great palace, and the lilting strains of "Pinafore" and the rest came softly to our ears. The king, with an accent more American than British, welcomed his guests with a gracious speech, a copy of which I obtained for the book. Again Mr. Davis scored with a masterful reply.

After the banquet, the king and queen made the "grand circle." We all repaired to an adjoining hall where the guests lined the four walls and waited for their majesties. I stood between the captain and the ship's navigator. It interested me to observe how well the king had prepared for this difficult function. It must have required hours of study to be able to speak with understanding to the varied types that made up the imposing circle. When he came to the Filipino members of the governor's cabinet he had an appropriate word for each. He discussed briefly agriculture, finances and social problems so expertly that it amazed the gentlemen from Manila.

When the king came to Captain Halsey Powell he inquired about the *Pittsburgh*. He knew as much about the old cruiser as I did. Then he came to me. He had been equally well coached, for he told me about his Catholic subjects. He praised their success in establishing schools and hospitals throughout the kingdom. He hoped our sailors were enjoying the sights in Bangkok. The little queen also had a word to say; she mentioned that their friend, the senior Douglas Fairbanks, had recently visited Bangkok on his way to the jungle to hunt wild animals. I admitted that one from Hollywood should feel quite at home in such an atmosphere—knowing Hollywood, the queen was amused.

With newspaper clippings, photographs, notes from Denebrink and sketches done by Fitch, I began to make up two dummies of the book. On our arrival at Singapore I sent one dummy by air mail to Chaplain Rentz with the plea that he camp at the publisher's door step and send me reports by radio. During the busy social week at Singapore, when the British army officers nearly wrecked us with their program of hospitality—tennis, golf, and dinner, at the various artillery posts—a dispatch from Rentz told me that the dummy had arrived and that the printers were already setting up the copy. He suggested a few changes, and for days we argued back and forth through the ether until an agreement was reached. It was certainly a fantastic way to make a book. As far as it concerned the material I was gathering, the book was three quarters finished before we sailed for Sumatra. I planned to have the whole of the second dummy in the air mail before we left Java. Our next stop was the island of Bali. Having been to Bali in the *Black Hawk,* I was able to anticipate happenings and write stories of events I felt would normally take place. It was a gamble, but we won. On the way from Sumatra, where we visited rubber plantations and saw the Dutch fire department of Medan dash to a real fire on bicycles—they even pedaled the hook-and-ladder truck and the hose-cart—I had everything for the book except the pictures and the story of crossing the Equator.

This event at sea was the high light of the cruise. The governor general was a good sportsman, winning the hearts of the men when he pleaded with Neptunus Rex to allow him to substitute for his daughter in the initiation ceremonies. Mr. Davis had already crossed the "line" but he patiently allowed the *Pittsburgh* shellbacks to lead him to the electrified platform where he danced when they turned on the "juice"; and he let them heave him into the tank where the polar bears "did their stuff."

With a pile of radio messages from Rentz on my desk, I sent by air mail from Batavia the second half of the book.

Dispatches continued coming and radio arguments prevailed until after our visit to Makassar in the Celebes. From there, when I returned from the topside motion picture show, most of the dispatches carried reassuring news of the progress.

To the amazement of my shipmates and my total delight, the book was ready when we reached Manila. Stacks of them were piled high on the dock, and I taxied to the governor's palace with an armful.

My friend, George Rentz, had done nobly in his job as liaison editor. We had published a book by air mail and radio. The men liked it.

The afternoon of our arrival at Manila Bay I took a boat to the *Black Hawk* just before they weighed anchor for Honk Kong, the first port of call on the long spring cruise to Chefoo, North China.

CHAPTER 33

Home Again

ONE night in August, 1931, Ching, my rickshaw boy who for two years had faithfully trotted me through the streets of Chefoo, gave me my last slow jog to the Bund. Behind him were two other rickshaw coolies pulling the freight. In their little two-wheelers, Ching had stacked the tennis gear and clothes I had kept in my room at the Chefoo Club. And behind this retinue came the Ray Tarbucks and my companion, "Dolly" Fitzgerald. These jolly friends came along to bid me *bon voyage*, for I had orders to leave in the morning in the *Simpson*. Her executive officer then was "Fitz" himself.

At the jetty, Ching immediately took charge. For the first time since I had employed him, he raised his voice in excitement, bossing the other coolies and directing them in the handling of the luggage. Ordinarily Ching's face was like a faded mask and his voice had no life to it. Mindful of the American's reputation for overpaying coolies and servants and the dismal charge that the Chinese working people are ungrateful anyway, I was determined to show Ching that I was especially pleased with his fidelity by giving him a good tip that he would long remember. He was different from the rest. Two years before, when he had spied me stepping out of the *Black Hawk* boat at the jetty, it happened; either he adopted me or it was the other way. The next time I came ashore, Ching fought his way through a group of shouting coolies, grabbed my tennis racket and told the whole coolie world I was his boss, and he did not mean maybe. He was the most unpromising one of the lot. His cut-off dungaree trousers had once graced the sturdy legs of a bluejacket. His ragged blue shirt was wide open to the belt, and he, unlike the others, wore no hat. That summer a few of us officers in a playful mood had our tailors fit out our rickshaw boys with fancy blouse and pants of Filipino drill. On the chest they wore our monograms. I gave Ching a Chinese dollar to buy a straw hat. Instead of a soft, comfortable, serviceable, fedora type of lid, the unique Ching somewhere unearthed a stiff brimmed sailor straw that "stopped the show." He was comical, but the hat made him easy to find, when I needed him. His only weakness was an inordinate fondness for garlic. Riding in his rickshaw became a chore until I confided in Fritz, the old German who ran a restaurant near the tennis club. Fritz, an old China hand, solved the problem by drawing up a contract that bound Ching to abstinence from garlic from sunrise to sunset. One afternoon Fritz solemnly led Ching to our table and had him draw the appropriate character on the dotted line. From then on I marked Ching's fitness report with a 4.0, which every sailor knows is "tops."

After paying off Ching's assistants, I called him to my side and made a speech of farewell. My friends gathered about as though we were putting on an act. In pidgin English I told the boy I was going "home-side"; I thanked him for his faithful services and added I hoped to see him again. Then I handed him the equivalent of four and one half gold dollars, a stupendous sum. Ching looked at me with an unfathomable expression, turned his back and walked away. I was hurt. It took the breath from me. Were the cynics really right after all in their estimate of the coolie? I looked across the bay and saw the *Black Hawk* motor launch approaching. As though nothing had happened I walked over to where my friends were standing. They had seen, and they sympathized. The boat came alongside in the dark. Two sailors jumped out to get my things, when I heard Ching's voice. "No, no, me catch Master's bags." He pushed the sailors aside and started down the steps with his arms loaded. At the end he came to me. Tears streamed down his leathery face. He put out his hand and said: "Thanks, Master. You go homeside. You come back. Ching, your boy." I patted the poor fellow on the back, but he pulled away and walked hurriedly to his rickshaw. I last saw him rounding the bend heading for home. I believe the Chinese are splendid people. Most of my friends are coolies. I am willing to take a chance on the others.

In Japan, where I spent a fortnight, I liked everything that was not imitation American. The days I spent in lovely Kyoto are lodged securely in my collection of aesthetic memories. The walks I took in the fairyland parks and the visits made to the red lacquered temples were inspiring; and I noted the reverence the people showed as they, dressed in their flowery kimonos, calmly entered their temples to pray.

The Japanese treated me with marked courtesy. Although I met no military people, I found the few civilians I spoke with, pleasant and anxious to make my visit a happy one. One morning I stood on the platform of a railway station, waiting for a train to Tokio. A professional-looking person, carrying a briefcase, came up to me and said in English, "Good morning, Sir. I believe you are an American. May I be of assistance?" Such courtesies prompted me at that time to like the Japanese.

The Dollar Liner made a fast passage in the fog to Seattle where I hastily boarded a train for Washington, D. C.

The husband of my sister, Anita, Commander Roger A. Nolan, was on duty then at the Naval Powder Factory at Indian Head, Maryland. I spent several days' leave in the bosom of that happy family. Father came down from Bethlehem while I was there. The Nolan children enjoyed the movie reels I had taken on my jaunt around the world. Jack, the eldest, had just entered the first grade in the village school. Anita, the only girl in the family, was just old enough to show her Uncle Bill how to walk like an elephant, proving that the postal cards she had received from the Dutch East Indies had educational value. Anita was born on the island of St. Croix when her father was on duty there. The tall and affectionate maid, Adelaide Gums, who came up from the Virgin Islands before Jack was born, called the little girl "Baba," meaning baby. To her brothers and her Uncle Bill she is still known as Baba. The baby in those days was Roger Michael; I found him impatiently waiting for his uncle to baptize him in the little country church, with my old *"Arkie"* shipmate, Finley France, who was on duty there, standing by to be godfather by proxy. Sergeant William Augustus Maguire Nolan, who with his brother, Lieutenant Mike, is now attending St. Catherine's Military School at Anaheim,

California, had not as yet joined the ranks of my favorite family.

After distributing among the members of the family the varied items of "loot" I had brought home from the Far East, I proceeded to demonstrate my luck by making a hole-in-one on the local links. I was one of a foursome made up of father, Dr. Nolan and Paymaster Harry Hines. At the ninth tee, when delayed by a foursome ahead of us, I said to my partner, Harry, a shipmate on the China Station, "Harry, for old times' sake I'll use an Asiatic ball for this shot." I dug deep in the bag's pocket and drew out a veteran that had weathered many a slice in Manila. To the faint annoyance of father, who was always a stickler for form, I wiggle-waggled like a clown, started my swing and hit the ball with the best follow-through I have ever achieved. It went straight and high over a tall barrier of trees and disappeared from sight. It looked as if I had overshot the green. But Hines had followed the ball. Arriving on the green we found it in the cup. It is now in a mahogany case which later on, the Dunlop Company generously provided. Doubting Thomases have read about the stunt in the Spalding Guide—for duffers, like myself.

With orders in my pocket, I motored to Philadelphia and reported to the commandant for duty in the Navy Yard. For three months, before I relieved Captain Bower R. Patrick as yard chaplain, I served as his assistant. The day he was detached, which marked the end of thirty years of service, he carried on as though it was his first day in the Navy. He handled a dozen or more difficult navy relief cases through the morning and visited the sick in every ward of the hospital in the afternoon. A few days after he left Philadelphia, he wrote me from the University of Chicago, where he had matriculated for a long course of study under professors who formerly had been his classmates. It was a pleasure to serve with Chaplain Patrick, for he was a living portrait of a sincere, conscientious and successful minister of his church.

As secretary and treasurer of the Navy Relief Society, I spent hours daily in my office and in the homes of the families of navy men aiding them in their domestic difficulties. The society, which was established on the proceeds of an Army-Navy football game, has for years been a boon to the navy enlisted personnel. It has given the chaplain corps an excellent opportunity for organized social service.

My colleague in the Yard was Chaplain Razzie W. Truitt. We had many interests in common, including a love for the national sport. One day a letter came inquiring how we stood in the matter of Sunday baseball. The City of Brotherly Love had at least one winning ball team whose playing the fans were by law forbidden to see on Sundays. With easy collaboration we explained the navy chaplain's point of view and we were awarded a pair of annual passes to the parks where the Athletics and the Phillies played. On many afternoons, although we arrived a bit late, we expressed our appreciation, in the grandstand.

Shore duty in Philadelphia was not unlike a sabbatical year from the sea, and I might have sought a billet afloat much sooner had not Father Gerald C. Treacy, S. J., my friend of the war days, been a professor in St. Joseph's College. During our many hours together it was apparent that he had not lost his interest in the apostolate of the

navy priest. When the *Dobbin*, the destroyer tender, came
to the Yard, I acquired an inseparable companion in
Father Thomas F. Regan. We spent our evenings together
and made frequent sorties to Indian Head where the popular padre won the hearts of the Nolan children. It was due
to the encouragement and aid of these estimable padres
that I was able to hold a military field Mass on Memorial
Day in 1932. It was well attended by service people, and
thousands who came to the Yard from town. Our preacher
was Monsignor Joseph M. Corrigan who then was rector
of Overbrook Seminary. He is now a bishop and rector
of the Catholic University in Washington. Assisting me,
the celebrant of the Mass were two former navy chaplains, Father Philip E. Donahue and Father Garret F.
Murphy. The altar was rigged on the porch of the marine
barracks, through the courtesy of the commanding officer,
my old friend and former "skipper," Lieutenant Colonel
Harold F. Wirgman, U.S.M.C.

In the spring of 1933 word reached me that my friend,
G. Barry Wilson, had recently joined the modernized and
newly commissioned *Mississippi*, fitting out in the Norfolk
Navy Yard. My natural dislike for shore duty and the
prospect of again being shipmates with my old friend of
the China Station, prompted me to request duty in the
"*Missy*." Our chief of the chaplain's division, Captain
Sydney K. Evans, who had always lent a sympathetic ear
to my requests, gave his approval.

With sea bag, suitcases and a merry heart, I motored
to the shores of Virginia.

CHAPTER 34

Aloha

THE great *Mississippi*, rebuilt from keel to truck, still retained the spirit in her ship's company that had won for her the name of the "Home Ship" of the Fleet. Her commanding officer, Captain William D. Puleston, was a stern disciplinarian but all hands knew how devoted he was to the task of making her an efficient unit in the battle line.

Shortly after we left the noisy Navy Yard in the fall of 1933, a dispatch from the Bureau of Operations sent us full speed to Havana to exert a peaceful influence on certain malcontents that were sowing the seeds of revolution. We rather enjoyed that, although we might have preferred a few liberties in that attractive Cuban city. When the ship arrived off Morro Castle, our battle flags were flying, guns were trained at maximum elevation, and our landing force of marines and armed bluejackets in their newly coffee-dyed uniforms, were assembled on the quarterdeck. All of Sunday and the following day the mighty *"Missy"* cruised close to the shoreline where the citizens promenading in the park could see that Uncle Sam wanted peace and safety for his nationals even though he had to shoot for it. Apparently our display of force was effective because Rear Admiral Charles S. Freeman, Commander of the Special Service Squadron, ordered the ship to proceed to

Dry Tortugas and stand by for developments. We faced, in that desolate spot on the empty sea, a hot, monotonous month. To keep the men amused we staged competitive deck sports on "Field Days Without Sand" a sly reference to the Friday job of scrubbing the decks with sand and generally cleaning the ship for inspection.

Lying at anchor, waiting for our Cuban neighbors to settle down, gave us a chance to think up ways to dramatize a program for the ship's morale.

In October the ship returned to Norfolk. We called the new ship's paper *The Pirate*. The thought behind the title had interesting possibilities. This I had realized a few months before, when a disturbing case of shingles impelled me to take a busman's holiday in the form of a sea trip to Boston where I had lunch with my old friend of the Brest days, Dr. Thomas Healy. That day in his club I met William Brown, the artist. With a definite ulterior motive I told him about the *Pirate* and how we intended to sell the idea of piratical energy to the crew by theatrical means. The ship was to set forth on a quest for "loot" in the form of trophies for excellence of performance in the Fleet. When I returned to the ship, the mail orderly delivered a package of Brown's pen-and-ink drawings of pirates. I took them to Barry Wilson and T. Starr King, the first lieutenant, and we went into a huddle. We chose the best of the lot which showed the profile of a particularly gruesome pirate aiming in dead earnest an enormous horse pistol. This became the insignia worn on the uniforms of the ship's athletes. Jack Tate, our senior aviator, had it painted on the ship's planes. The men liked the idea and the officers also became enthusiastic.

My old friends of fleet air days, Eva and Jimmie Dyer,

were living at the air station. One evening, Barry Wilson and I called and told them in mock seriousness that the "*Missy*," which had once been Jimmie's ship, was to better the record of former days because we had acquired a new determination to excel under the inspiration of piratical ruthlessness. But there were difficulties. If only we had pirate costumes for the ship's band. This was mentioned for Eva's especial interest. We rather felt that she would quickly volunteer to shop for material and have her seamstress make boleros, sashes and bandanas for the ship's bandsmen. The large brass buttons on the black boleros shone like doubloons of the Spanish Main. The silk sashes and bandanas to match, were in green, gold and red. With a white shirt and bell-bottom trousers the costume was complete. Eva had not failed us.

That winter at Guantanamo Bay, Cuba, the night we went ashore to the station arena to give battle to the boxers and wrestlers of our sister ship, the *New Mexico*, the sailors wondered what had become of the "*Missy*" band, when suddenly they heard the distant sound of a bugle, and saw a gang of pirates marching over a near-by hill. Preceding the ship's band, resplendent in their new costumes, marched a dozen pirates carrying flaming torches and yelling spasmodically, "Yo ho! Yo ho! Yo ho!" When our pirates entered the arena, I shook with emotion. It took me several minutes to realize how funny it was to be so worked up over this childish amusement. But it did something to our crew, especially the men in the ring. That night they put on a raid for "loot" that would have satisfied the greed of a Sir Henry Morgan. They won every bout.

The new *Mississippi* joined the Fleet at Panama and

took part, a few months later, in the presidential review off Sandy Hook. In New York, the captain and the executive officer, Commander Charles E. Reordan, were relieved by Captain Sam Loomis and Commander Francis W. Rockwell. In the autumn of 1934, the Fleet returned to Southern California.

We took aboard five hundred recruits at Norfolk. There were so many new men in our crew that it was not easy to reach the standards of the Fleet. The men worked hard at drills, however, and I feel that our efforts to dramatize the ship's spirit had much to do with the *Mississippi's* fine performance later on in engineering and gunnery. Our athletes held their own, and the pirate orchestra charmed the ladies.

In the spring of 1935, on our return from Fleet maneuvers in Hawaiian waters, orders came sending me to the training station at Newport, Rhode Island. Again, after thirteen years in fields afar, I helped put in commission the historic training school for sailors. During the financial depression the station had been closed. It was interesting but strenuous work. To transform a happy-go-lucky, undisciplined American boy into a dependable man-o'-war's man is for me second in importance only to serving with them in our ships.

At the end of my fifth month at Newport, the medicos decided that I, like an old battle-wagon, was in need of an overhaul. They put me to bed and kept me there for six weeks and then suggested that I might join my relatives in California, where the doctors in San Diego could decide whether or not "my number was up" for retirement. To my complete satisfaction the Bureau ordered my friend, Father Vincent J. Gorski, to relieve me as senior chaplain of the training station. "Vince" came hurriedly from the cruiser, *Astoria*, based in the Pacific. They could not have placed my job in more capable hands. Father Gorski has a special genius for work with navy men; he is beloved ashore and afloat by all hands.

While living in the foot hills beyond San Diego, father died suddenly. After his death I started to build a home on the top of a knoll, about ten miles from the sea. I designed it after an old Mexican hacienda I knew, and watched the builders every day, while on sick leave, as they put together the place where I expected to spend the rest of my days. My little niece Anita, alias "Baba," who found it impossible to live in her parents' home in Coronado because the sea air brought on attacks of asthma, came to live with me. She brought with her Esme, the niece of Adelaide Gums, the beloved "Mammy" of the Nolan family. We took possession of the hacienda and christened it "Casa de Anita." My mother's name was Ann; her only daughter, my sister, was named Anita (little Ann) and her only daughter, in turn, was given the name which I thought would be appropriate for the dwelling father had made possible for the years of my retirement.

Baba, Esme, and I, with our two cocker spaniels, Happy and Lucky, lived for two years in our hilltop home. There, whether it was due to the skill of the doctors or to the prayers of the Carmelite nuns of San Diego, I regained my health. The Bureau then ordered me back to duty at the local training station. Of course I was happy to be in the Navy again.

Those were peculiarly happy years in this unusual setting. I soon became aware of all I had missed in the many years I had spent at sea where you cannot plant trees and rose bushes and learn to love them intimately. It was a quarter of a century since I had lived in a home. It was the first time I had *ever* lived in a home of my own where I had full and pleasing responsibility. My little niece, who was then nine, needed the gentle care of her West Indian maid, but she came to her Uncle Bill for private lessons in the three R's until she was well enough to enter the grammar school in La Mesa. My new duties in the home improved my outlook on the world. The experience was most enjoyable and beneficial.

Whenever I had guests for dinner my little niece dressed in Spanish costume and acted as hostess. She will never forget the dinner party we gave Bishop Charles F. Buddy when she served the biscuits and spilled them in the bishop's lap.

My colleagues at the training station were Chaplains Harrill S. Dyer, and Razzie W. Truitt. Razzie and I had been together in the Philadelphia Navy Yard. He joined me at the training station when Harrill went to sea. It was fine to be with him again. Dyer and I had served in the Fleet for several years but this was our first shore duty together. He and his wife, the talented Louise, often came to the Casa where Louise interested my niece in our new piano while Harrill and I reviewed events of the day.

On Sunday mornings my little niece accompanied me to the station. The round trip of twenty-five miles and the two Masses she attended made up a rather heavy schedule for a little girl of nine. She helped dress the altar, and after the second Mass she attended the children's catechism class. When the morning's work was done, we had breakfast in the officers' club, where Chaplain Dyer usually joined us. I would steer the conversation to a discussion of our sermons in order to learn how mine had impressed my "little shipmate." Her criticism was so natural and frank that I finally made it a regular routine procedure. One day she said, "Uncle Bill, you spoke today as if you were angry. You pounded the pulpit, and I don't think the sailors liked it. Why don't you talk like you do at home?" At times she would ask, "Why don't you tell them more stories, Uncle Bill? Now that was a good story you told this morning about the poor Chinese children on the golf course near Hong Kong, picking up the grasshoppers to make soup with. Stories like that make your sermon so much better." If my talks to navy men have improved since then, I have Baba to thank for her simple words of wisdom at our Sunday morning critiques.

The important event of that tour of duty at the training station was the military field Mass we held on Memorial Day of 1937 when we honored the first Bishop of San Diego, the Most Reverend Charles F. Buddy, D.D., who presided and preached the sermon. All the officers and their families and four thousand recruits, and a thousand or so marines from the marine base, and thousands of civilians from town, filled one of the patios. A special place in the balconies was reserved for the parochial school Sisters. My friend of the Brest days, Colonel Philip Torrey, now a major general, was in command of the marines. A large choir of civilians, specially rehearsed for the occasion, sang at the Mass and a w.p.a. orchestra played the accompaniment. Bishop Buddy was deeply impressed by the coöperation given by Captain Paul P. Blackburn, the commanding officer of the station and by his staff. It was for me an inspiring demonstration and it increased my respect and affection for the Navy.

Orders came in the spring of 1938 detaching me from the training station and assigning me to the heavy cruiser *Indianapolis* with additional duty on the staff of the commander scouting force, as force chaplain. When I reported on board, Vice Admiral William T. Tarrant was the force commander, and Captain Thomas C. Kinkaid was in command of the flagship. They were soon to leave. The admiral left to command the First Naval District at Boston and the captain to Rome as naval attaché. Our executive officer, Commander Oscar C. Badger, was ordered to the Naval War College. By the middle of summer Vice Admiral Adolphus Andrews had become the force commander and Captain John F. Shafroth, Jr., a shipmate of the *Arkansas* days, assumed command of the ship. The new executive officer, Commander Ralph O. Davis, made life aboard the *Indianapolis* especially enjoyable. We had many mutual friends and I got to know him intimately as I had his classmates Oliver "Scrappy" Kessing and Barry Wilson. On cruises we usually went ashore together; on board I found it a joy to assist him in problems regarding the welfare of the crew. The heavy cruiser reminded me of the *Idaho* when she was new; there was an atmosphere of smartness in the ship herself and in the performance of the ship's company. With a distinguished admiral and staff as shipmates and with the sterling leadership of the ship's officers, the ship had an excellent esprit de corps.

When the second World War impelled the Navy to break out the war plans for national defense, a group of fast, hard-striking ships were formed into a new organization called the Hawaiian Detachment. With Vice Admiral Adolphus Andrews in command, we put to sea in October, 1939, for Hawaiian waters. The *Indianapolis* was due at this time for a major overhaul in the Bremerton Navy Yard, so the admiral and staff moved to the carrier, *Enterprise*. My old friend, Alfred D. Vogler, was the ship's chaplain. The admiral agreed that it would be better that I go along in a ship that had no chaplain. I chose the cruiser, *Northampton*. She was the flagship of Rear Admiral John H. Newton; her commanding officer, Captain Samuel S. Payne.

The people of Honolulu suddenly realized that eleven thousand officers and men had come to stay. How to meet the new situation became a serious civic problem. To provide transportation to town when the men swarmed ashore on liberty, and how to take care of them when they got there, gave the city fathers a hard nut to crack. Facilities for athletics and amusement near the Yard were inadequate for so many.

In the *Northampton* we discovered enough talented men to stage a revue. For many days at sea we rehearsed in the officers' country and finally had something worthy of a name. We called the revue "The Northampton Follies" and ran it four nights during Christmas week. The first night we gave it on board the cruiser for the enlisted men; the second night we invited the vice admiral, officers and ladies; the third night we took the troupe to the carrier *Enterprise* where we entertained three thousand on the hangar deck; the last night the *Northampton* thespians took over the theatre of the Navy Yard Y.M.C.A. Lieutenant Commander John "Jerry" O'Donnell was my able partner from the start. We labored under the usual seagoing handicaps but we came through with colors flying. As a result of our *Northampton* experiment we combined the talent of all the ships of the Hawaiian Detachment and organized the "Hawdet Variety Troupe." Then we gave several performances on the 10–10 dock, entertaining thousands of our homesick sailors.

In the spring of 1940, when the Pacific Fleet came down to the Islands, no one dreamed they had come to stay. It meant that sixty thousand more joined the personnel of the Hawaiian Detachment to put further strain on the community. Plans were immediately drawn up to provide recreation centers near the Navy Yard. In the fall of 1941, these excellent projects were completed. But in spite of the Bloch Recreation Center, the Richardson Fleet pool at Aiea, of Camp Andrews at Nanakuli Beach, and the newly commissioned swimming facilities at Barber's Point, the men continued to go to town for recreation. Honolulu still faced a heavy problem.

When American sailors are cruising on the high seas, there is so much to do of an exacting kind that they have little time to think about themselves or to feel sorry for themselves. They know today that drills are not simply book-rules put into action; they feel that these are but brief rehearsals of a show that for their ship may mean, at some time, success or death. But it was quite a different story when the Pacific Fleet returned to Pearl Harbor and liberty call was sounded. From the Navy Yard it is a ride of nearly ten miles to Honolulu. And there was not much for a sailor to do after he got there. He had already gone on the chaplain's round-the-island-sightseeing-party; he had visited the aquarium, the pineapple factory and Bishop's Museum. The beach at Waikiki is still another long bus ride from the heart of town. In these circumstances a young sailor could become discouraged.

Friends of mine recently discovered a young fellow sitting in solitary doldrums on a rock at far-away Koko Head where the sea waves were breaking. An elderly lady in a party of motorists feared the boy might be in distress. She had the driver stop the car and asked, "Son, can we do anything for you?"

The lonely man-o'-war's man turned his head and sadly replied, "No, thank you, Ma'am." Then he turned his eyes again toward the billowy horizon and with his head in his hands he complained: "I'm just looking at San Francisco."

Now, in 1941, I am Fleet Chaplain of the Pacific Fleet, serving on the staff of the Commander Battle Force, Vice Admiral William S. Pye, U.S.N. Ordinarily I should be serving on board the flagship *California*, but the admiral has assigned me to duty in Honolulu to coördinate the work of civilians in the interest of the welfare of the men of the Fleet. In March, 1941, the Army and Navy Y.M.C.A., through their director, Mr. Wesley Wilke, gave me and my three yeomen, Lee Durbin, "Mike" Striebel and Joseph Workman, an office where for the past ten months I have worked with the Mayor's Entertainment Committee, headed by Mrs. J. Platt Cooke and Miss Nell Findley. When the people of Honolulu—individuals and societies— wish to entertain men of the Fleet, they first consult with the Mayor's Committee and then the invitations are distributed among the soldiers and sailors based on the Island of Oahu. It is my job to assign allocations to the forces afloat and to arrange for transportation.

The vast majority of our men abhor the cheap allurements of the local saloons. They much prefer the sort of party the Catholic Ladies Aid frequently gives for over one hundred Fleet men. Buses, which the Navy hire with our welfare funds, take the men to the Capitol grounds whence the women drive them in their cars over the Pali to the country estates of the Dillinghams, the Carters, the Castles and the Cookes. They enjoy swimming, games and the home-cooked chow which the women bring. A band from one of the battleships usually goes along and plays for the dancing. The Honolulu Hostess Committee has been entertaining with a swank formal dance twice a month at the beautiful Ala Moana Pavilion where the men meet the loveliest girls in town and dance under the stars. The men appreciate the tone and refinement that always prevails. Recently the young business women organized what they call "The Flying Squadron." They make weekly flights to army posts and the navy club house at Aiea for an evening of dancing.

The people of Honolulu have been truly hospitable to the men of the armed forces. The most important form of entertainment takes place in the homes. Along with frequent picnics at houses on the beach, supper parties in town are given to smaller groups. Men are invited to concerts and dramatic programs staged by racial organizations of the city. Pageants have been specially put on by the Chinese, Japanese, Hawaiians and Koreans. The high schools invite the men to hear their a capella choirs; the university gives special performances enacted by the Theatre Guild; the Honolulu Community Theatre invites hundreds of men to their dress rehearsals.

The Mayor's Entertainment Committee has become the nucleus for the newly organized United Services Organization (U.S.O.). They have organized the community for the many and varied activities which will be conducted for the men of the armed forces and the thousands of civilian workers who have lately come to Oahu. The first bishop of the diocese of Honolulu, the Most Reverend James J. Sweeney, D.D., soon after his installation organized the Catholic unit of the U.S.O. The bishop has taken a lively interest in the welfare of the men of the armed forces.

I am now in the middle of my twenty-fourth year of service as a navy chaplain and I feel that my present assignment is a natural culmination of years of this sort of week-day work. As a chaplain it always seemed natural that I should be busy with smokers, Happy Hours, dramatics, athletics, sightseeing parties to complement the more specifically religious functions of my navy apostolate. Most of the chaplain's work aboard ship is spent in personal interviews with the men, but he can and does achieve worthy results by promoting recreational activity of the sort that endows the young man-o'-war's man with a *"mens sana in corpore sano."*

A few days ago a young man with a leaning toward pacifism asked me why I joined the Navy, why I was so anxious to go overseas in the last war. Was it the spirit of adventure or hatred for the enemy? I believe he is so like many others who do not understand the life mission of a Catholic priest. Unfortunately, there are many Americans who fail to understand the supernatural motive that inspires a priest in his holy mission. They do not know that a priest goes into battle for the sole purpose of administering the Sacraments to the dying and to bolster the courage of those about to face death. A priest serves in our Spartan ships of war because he yearns to reach the hearts of men to keep alive there the Faith of Our Fathers.

I once wrote an article for the *Ecclesiastical Review* in which I said, "Looking back over the years, what with serving in the Grand Fleet at Scapa Flow, in the war-zone destroyers, in ships bound on diplomatic missions to South America, the Black Sea, to Siam and Java and the China Station, I feel that I have had my share of glamour. But I believe now that it was pretty much a chore and simply a splendid opportunity to offer Mass and to preach the word of God to those who otherwise would have been deprived. Those days at sea were hallowed by the reenactment of the mystical Calvary and the happy return of navy men to their duties with the grace of God in their hearts . . . A priest who sets his heart on a career in the Navy because he yearns for brass buttons, gold braid and a 'look-see' at the world will be sadly fooled, completely disillusioned and—may God forbid—whipped . . ." In another place I said, "For the Chaplain there is always the consoling conviction, should he ever feel discouraged, that he is giving at least as much to his apostolate as any secular priest of his acquaintance. The work is difficult, but the opportunities to serve God are boundless. What more could one want?"

The chaplains of the Army and Navy today are fortunate in having as their spiritual superiors the Most Reverend Francis J. Spellman, D.D., Archbishop of New York—Military Vicar, and the Most Reverend John F. O'Hara, D.D., Military Delegate. Bishop O'Hara has mastered our problem. The Holy Father could not have chosen an abler leader.

It has given me great happiness these many years to respond to my vocation with a cheerful navy, "Aye, aye."

As I write the final words of this book of memories I wish you who have traveled so far with me "Aloha Nui." It is Saturday, December 6, 1941. I am about to pack my Mass kit and study the Epistle and Gospel for tomorrow's Mass. My ship is in port. Tomorrow at 7:30 A.M. my yeoman, Joseph Francis Workman, will accompany me to the navy yard; a staff motor boat will pick us up at the Officers' Club landing. I shall offer Mass on the forecastle, for the trade winds are blowing and the weather will be clear.

CHAPTER 35

December Seventh

WITH one of my yeomen, Joseph Workman, Seaman Second Class, who usually carries my Mass kit, I stood on the Officers' Club landing at Pearl Harbor on Sunday, December 7, 1941, waiting for a staff motor boat to take us to the flagship where I was scheduled to hear confessions at eight-thirty and offer Mass on the forecastle at nine.

As we stood there in the cool of a stiff trade wind, admiring the perfection of a Hawaiian morning, fluffy clouds skirted the verdant mountain tops, and the varied hues of green of the plantations below delighted the eye. Making a mental note regarding the wind, I decided to ask the officer of the deck to have the working party rig a wind-break lest my altar things be blown over the side. It was an especially bright and fresh morning. (It was so different the following day when we experienced the worst weather in my two and a half years on Oahu.) I remarked to my cheerful yeoman, "Joe, this is one for the tourist."

Just then, as the motor boat approached the landing, I spied a flock of light carrier planes that resembled our own. They dove vertically, dropping bombs on ships moored at 10–10 dock. To Workman, I said, "They're phoney bombs, full of flour or something. But, they've picked a swell time for a sham battle." Before I heard the bombs explode, a plane, painted a dirty mustard color, zoomed out of the sun across my right shoulder. It carried a steel torpedo that glistened. The plane levelled out about twenty feet above the water, and headed for a battleship, dropped the torpedo and pulled up sharply, nearly hitting the upper works.[1] Following instantly came another plane. We spied the round patch of blood red on the fuselage. Then the din of the bombs and a great geyser near the ship. The shock made me strangely sick. All I could say was, "We're in it. We're in it." After the first wave of planes I ordered the coxswain to make the gangway of a destroyer which was moored to a dock close by. It seemed in the circumstances to be the correct thing to do. This was a new kind of traffic jam. The men in the boat were cool. One lad, half to himself, remarked, "Can it be possible? They're Japs!"

By the time we climbed aboard where a young lieutenant met us, the sky-guns of all the ships were blazing away at the treacherous enemy. Our men were quick getting to their batteries. The lieutenant asked me quite calmly to keep the men of our boat and the crew of a motor launch under cover. Shrapnel was falling. A moment later he gave me a raincoat to wear. He said, "Your white uniform may draw their fire."

---

[1] Little did I dream then that that ship later became the tomb of my dear friend, Father Schmitt. May God rest his soul. I discovered later that my friend, Chaplain Thomas L. Kirkpatrick lost his life in his ship. He was to relieve me this winter as fleet chaplain. May he be granted eternal peace.

The din made by our guns and the exploding bombs was deafening. High overhead came groups of five high altitude bombers. As I looked up at them, Workman called my attention to a diving plane that had dropped its torpedo prematurely. It was about fifty feet above the water, just beyond the club landing, when the guns of our ship scored a hit. The plane exploded in a great flash. The wooden wreckage of the wings and fuselage covered the water near us. The men were all for picking up the pieces for souvenirs. But they were sensibly denied the privilege. This may have been their way of showing they had no fear; they were merely taking a lively interest in the proceedings.

To see the horrible show on the other side of the ship I crossed the deck and noticed two sailors standing on the dock, shouting. I waved them aboard and asked what they wanted. One said, "Our ship is out of commission, Sir. Bein' overhauled. We'd like to help out." I told them to report to the bridge for orders and "chop chop." They were fine lads. I shall never forget the expressions on their faces. It feels good to be playing on their team, for they are certainly warriors of the first water.

The young lieutenant again came to me after the final wave of torpedo planes and said he was soon to get under way but he added that he would not cast off before telling me. I knew there must be work for me in my own ship.

After twenty minutes or more on board the destroyer, while the high altitude bombers were passing overhead, I decided it was time to go to the flagship. Although the ship had been hit, we found no confusion on topside. The anti-aircraft guns were making it miserable for the enemy. I rather hoped to find in my room some cotton for my ears.

I lay below and found men calmly manning their stations. On the wardroom deck many wounded lay still. In the chief of staff's cabin I found several more; they said they were comfortable. Some one gave me a gas mask, and I went to my room to get a life-jacket. A steady stream of men, grimy with sweat and smeared with oil, carried boxes of ammunition to the hatchways and up the ladders to the guns. It was no picnic.

After an hour or more, orders came to remove the wounded. We carried them up the ladders and placed them gently in a motor launch for a quick trip to the air station. I missed that trip but when I again got to the quay I got aboard a motor whaleboat which we promptly filled with wounded and took them to the air station dispensary. Except for the grim presence of the suffering men the job was like a drill. On our second return to the ship the burning oil on the water drove us to the beach. After wading ashore, in the oil-covered water, my white uniform ceased to be a target. Nor was I a pretty picture.

Attending the wounded and dying became then a major task. My other yeoman, the capable Lee Durbin, Yeoman First Class, joined me at this time and he and Workman went with me on the rounds of the barrack rooms where the wounded lay on mess tables. Early in the afternoon I suddenly discovered why I felt a bit done in. Still fasting since midnight the day before, I was, as it were, on my way to celebrate Mass. Durbin got me a cup of coffee, and I confess we both worked up a smile over it.

The senior medico of the ship, Dr. Jesse D. Jewell, although badly burned, worked tirelessly for the wounded. When the situation was particularly unpromising and the Japs were strafing the barracks, little Mrs. Thomas A.

Christopher, a mother of small children, the wife of a former shipmate, an aviator, came to me and said, "I'm a registered nurse. I've come to help." She then began assisting Dr. Jewell. Mrs. Christopher quickly proved to be an angel of mercy.

When Dr. Jewell said he felt he should evacuate immediately at least one hundred men, I offered to take a boat and go to the Naval Hospital and inquire if they had room for them. Durbin and I jumped into a motor whaleboat, commandeered a car and sped to the hospital. On our return to the air station I asked the officer who had the day's duty to round up all available trucks and to hold the ferry. Placing the wounded on mattresses on the floor of the fifteen trucks we got aboard the ferry and crossed the bay to Merry Point Landing. From there the wounded were taken to three hospitals. By sun down all the wounded were evacuated from the air station.

Having run across Father Tom Odlum at the Naval Hospital, I knew that the men I had missed would receive from him the last rites. It was now time to report to the Chief of Staff and tell him what had been done.

I am deeply proud of my shipmates. Every one deserves an unreserved "Well done!"

INDEX